Unlock Your

CAREER SUCCESS

**KNOWING THE UNWRITTEN RULES
CHANGES EVERYTHING**

Christine
Brown-Quinn

R3THINK PRESS

First published in Great Britain in 2020 by Rethink Press (www.rethinkpress.com)

Cover image © Shutterstock | okart

Praise

'Christine Brown-Quinn's latest book, *Unlock Your Career Success*, is a pragmatic and incisive read for women at all stages of their career. What's refreshing about Christine is that she writes as she talks, speaking from real experiences, with stories and anecdotes that are both accessible and directly applicable.'

> – **Rebecca Robins**, Global Chief Learning and Culture Officer, Interbrand

'*Unlock Your Career Success* empowers women with truth-telling facts from the real business world paired with practical advice and insider knowledge that will help them to be promoted to the top. A compelling step by step manual enabling women to unleash their full potential without losing sight of their authenticity. This book shows women how to master the unwritten rules to climb the career ladder and stay on the fast track. Essential and inspiring reading for every working woman to realise their ambitions and aspirations.'

> – **Michaela Jedinak**, fashion designer and entrepreneur

'An exceptional human, insightful and engaging read. Even a degree from an Ivy League University doesn't guarantee us success in our career planning or business launch. Christine Brown-Quinn's book is the ultimate guide for the dynamic, determined and entrepreneurial woman who wants to know about the 'unwritten rules of success' and be at the top of her game!'

> – **Elizabeth Filippouli**, founder & CEO, Global Thinkers Forum & Athena40

'Recommended to all those who wish to make a success of their career and to realise their full potential. Christine has been delivering inspiring webinars for IWE since 2013. Her sound advice and top tips, based not only on her personal experience but also on the experience of others who have achieved success in their careers, has helped thousands around the world on their chosen career path over the years. This book will enable many more people to benefit from her knowledge.'

— **Peta Payne**, Managing Director, International Women of Excellence (IWE)

'A book packed with the advice and guidance I wish I had had earlier in my career to help navigate the corporate jungle, from someone who has lived, survived and succeeded.'

— **Bev Shah**, founder of City Hive

'Reading this book feels like being mentored by a no-nonsense, intuitive-yet-strategically-minded colleague. When it comes to networking, Christine debunks the myth painting it as a necessary evil and instead encourages the reader to focus on the relationships at its heart. She illustrates her points with convincing real-life scenarios, and her message becomes clear: invest in nurturing your connections today and they will work hard for you when you need them. This may be a book for the career-minded, but in essence it is an empathically-driven exploration of relationship-building in the world of business. A must-read.'

– **Alisa Grafton**, Partner,
Cheeswrights LLP

'Another thought-provoking title by Christine Brown-Quinn. Her many years' experience has been distilled into ten simple rules that are applicable to each of us, irrespective of job title or position. No matter whether as an author, speaker or coach, Christine poses simple yet thought- provoking questions that give us the chance to reflect on scenarios from an alternative perspective. Using her approach should give us the confidence to tackle familiar career challenges differently. The beauty of this book is the content can be digested in full or by individual chapter depending on your own situation. In my view, it is a must-have read to always have in easy reach.'

– **Raine Hunt**, Director of
Marketing & Communications,
Sopra Steria/NHS SBS

*I dedicate this book to my three children,
Sarah, Matt and Zach, who inspire
me to be my best self for others.*

Contents

Foreword   1

Introduction   3

Rule #1 – Claim Your Career   7

Think strategically   9

You are the business   12

Strategy is the foundation for stepping
up   14

Stepping outside your comfort zone   16

Moving up the food chain   18

Focus on strategic outcomes   22

Rule #2 – Crack The Confidence Code   27

We live in a new normal   28

Strive for confidence and competence
in equal measure   31

Tap into your courage memory bank   32

Curb the confidence killers   34

Taking imperfect action is a game-changer 38

Career breaks build confidence 43

Rule #3 – Prime Your Personal Brand 47

Your brand permeates your personal business plan 48

Build your brand using the CODE formula 50

Strengthen your brand through consistency 58

Enjoy the benefits of promoting your brand 61

Be ready to showcase your brand at any time 64

Rule #4 – Nourish Your Network 67

Career success depends on your ability to network 68

Set an objective for your networking strategy 71

Starting with why empowers your networking strategy 75

Networking is the bridge to tomorrow 76

What's your story 79

Turning networking into career opportunities 82

Rule #5 – Revere Relationships   **89**

We choose people we know and trust   90

Evaluate relationships through your
strategic lens   92

The difference between coaches,
mentors and sponsors   94

How to use mentors   96

How to use sponsors   99

Making the initial approach   102

It's a two-way street   104

Rule #6 – Navigate Negotiations   **111**

Asking changes everything   114

Know what's important to you   120

Prepare for likely objections   121

Align interests to build rapport   123

Be sure to benchmark your requests   125

Know your bottom line   127

Leveraging outcomes   128

**Rule #7 – Cherish Challenging
Conversations**   **133**

Difficult conversations lead to a
pathway of growth   134

Preparing for talks on pay and
promotion   137

Be your best self 139

Share the wider context 142

What doesn't kill you makes you stronger 143

Rule #8 – Deal With Difficult People 153

Behaviour breeds behaviour 154

Keep your cool 159

Listen actively 161

Mind your body language 164

Shift the focus to them 165

Prepare your response 166

Rule #9 – Tackle Tricky Tensions 173

Evaluate what to say yes to 174

Beware of the downside of not saying no 177

Focus on the outcome rather than the approach 179

Crafting an effective request 181

Make your requests motivational 183

Raising awkward issues 186

Standing your ground 188

Rule #10 – Manage Your Manager 193

Own the relationship 194

Make your boss successful 197

Approach your relationship as a
partnership   203
Managing conflict – agree to disagree   205
Establish mutual expectations   207

Final Thoughts   **213**

Acknowledgements   **215**

The Author   **217**

Foreword

A career is like a river or stream. At the beginning of your journey, you're never exactly certain where it will take you. It may be blocked and diverted, but it can also be refreshed and renewed – if you're willing to take risks. I've learned this important lesson in a communications career spanning forty years. During my journey I made a conscious decision to create my own unique style of professionalism and leadership, which was in stark contrast to the style of the frighteningly powerful moguls in broadcasting and publishing by whom I was surrounded. My experience has shown that you can achieve the outcomes you want through a smarter, intentional and strategic approach, rather than simply through heavy-handedness. Don't be mistaken: while my leadership style could be described as 'light touch', it has been every bit as effective in ensuring my voice has been heard and the required hard results achieved.

In this book Christine Brown-Quinn reveals key truths about how to lead an authentic life, personally and professionally, such as by taking full ownership of your career (including the diversions) as well as getting out of your comfort zone.

It is easy to see how Brown-Quinn has succeeded in a tough world. What we have here is far more than a 'how-to' manual; this book is designed to turn ambition and inspiration into success. Brown-Quinn's quality of thought serves to demystify the details of the process. I for one could have used such insight forty years ago!

The 'Brown-Quinn' style is clear, thought-provoking and inspirational, and likely to influence a new range of thinking about the 'career journey', far beyond a simple notion of success.

Geraldine Sharpe-Newton
Global communications strategist and mentoring advocate

Introduction

'If only I had known about the unwritten rules earlier, Christine, I could have been CEO!' These were the exact words used by my client Michelle* to describe her career history. She was frustrated that she only learned late in the game what really mattered when it came to her career progression, yet at the same time acknowledged how powerful this new information had been in catapulting her career in banking to the next level.

Since launching my career consultancy, The Female Capitalist®, in 2010, I have heard similar comments from thousands of women across the globe. Personally, I too could have experienced career success more quickly had I known earlier about the so-called 'soft skills' which are career

---

* The stories contained in this book about clients and colleagues are factual but the names have been changed in order to respect their privacy.

critical. It felt like a well-kept secret, and it was only when my career progression began to stall that I realised there was more to getting ahead than just doing a brilliant job. I had to figure out why I wasn't the one getting picked for the juicy projects, the big promotion and the hefty pay rise.

It's time to bust one of the biggest myths when it comes to career success: there is no such thing as a one-dimensional meritocracy. If you think that just by doing a good job you are going to get tapped on the shoulder for that next promotion, you'll likely be waiting a long time. Early on in my career I trusted wholeheartedly (and in retrospect blindly) that my managers would see my outstanding work and that would be all I needed to do. I believed that simply by working hard, my career would take off. I've had to learn the hard way that this is not true. My aim for writing this book is to share with you what's really going on when it comes to career progression so that you can achieve the success you want (and deserve) sooner rather than later.

The *real* secret to career success is not to do a stellar job at the exclusion of other truly career-enhancing behaviours. In this book I unveil the *unwritten* rules to career progression and then demonstrate through personal stories (my own as well as those of the many women I have had the privilege of coaching) how to navigate those rules in a practical and authentic way. Here's the thing... the same rules apply to men and women, but when women use the same *approach* to navigating those rules they suffer backlash. Have you ever been described as 'too aggressive' or 'acting like a b**ch'?

My years of experience as a coach and mentor reveal that once women understand the unwritten rules – with a little guidance and support – they perform magnificently. I am inspired by the thousands of women I've had the honour to work with who have experienced significant success by tweaking and prioritising their approach. It's not about completely reinventing yourself. You are a busy woman. I have no intention of adding to your (dreaded) to-do list. I will, however, help you consider doing things a little differently, focusing on the things that truly matter and will help you get to where you want to go.

Just to clarify, this book is not for or about superwomen. It's for normal, hard-working, smart women like you, who want to enjoy their career and still be true to themselves as well as have a personal life. Additionally, the unwritten rules I refer to apply to all organisational life. The rules apply regardless of whether you work in business, academia, or the not-for-profit sector. Even though there will be nuances in the individual culture and environments across organisations, sectors and geographies, the unwritten rules are still relevant as they relate to one common factor: human behaviour.

My hope is that this book empowers women as individuals to embrace their careers and unlock the success and fulfilment they deserve. It is only one part, however, of the multifaceted approach necessary to increase gender diversity in the workplace. Empowerment of the individual is not meant as a panacea, nor a substitute for the focus and effort of organisations to foster a culture where female talent is recognised, embraced and leveraged for tangible results.

Claim Your Career

There is a fairly straightforward formula for career success: hard work and delivering quality results. One of the most misunderstood issues in building a career is the belief in a one-dimensional meritocracy. Yet so many of us simply keep our heads down and do a great job, believing we will eventually be recognised for our talents. The truth is that in order to enjoy the career you want to have and deserve you've got to claim it. This is the case more today than ever before, as we work in an environment where the old way of doing things is being disrupted. Change is the only thing that is constant. Restructurings, reorganisations, and shifts in strategy are commonplace.

Are you experiencing some sort of change – perhaps a new boss, a more complex matrix reporting structure, or new and increased responsibilities – while your salary and title remain unchanged? Perhaps you've just figured out how to do your job when a brand-new cast of characters arrives for you to please, and they aren't really interested in the past. What you may not realise is that your managers are grappling with their own issues in this uncertain environment, which explains why they don't seem to be interested in your career development. It's nothing personal. During an interview at this year's French Tennis Open, British female number one Jo Konta was asked what the secret was to her recent success. She explained that she and her new coach are working well together and that while he may suggest strategies for her training and match prep, she's the one who owns her decisions on and off the court. Whether you're a world-class athlete or a business professional, it's only when you take full responsibility for your behaviour, actions and mindset that you're able to reach your true potential. You have to take ownership of your career.

Think strategically

No one knows you better than you, and by owning your future, you can shape it in a way that suits you best – keeping in mind of course the broader opportunities and trends happening in your organisation and industry. There is an easy way to go about this without adding more hours to your already long day, but it does require a fresh approach and a new way of thinking. While your company, your boss, human resource representative and career counsellor may take an interest in your career development, *you* are the one who is ultimately responsible. That doesn't mean you shouldn't ask for support and guidance from your manager or other colleagues in your company – you absolutely should. *You*, however, must be in the driving seat. You know where your interests lie, what energises you, and which personal goals and desires need to be met for you to be happy and fulfilled.

Thinking strategically requires you to raise your head above your laptop and come up for air. Listen to what others are chatting about. What's the *new* strategy? What's the latest development? Always have your eyes and ears open to hear what's most important to the organisation and then align yourself with this. Managing your career requires the same approach. Just doing the task at hand without looking up from your screen is a dangerous strategy. While you're busy executing your tasks to perfection, the world around you is evolving and the value of the work you are executing so beautifully may be decreasing. Always look to move up the value chain by focusing on what's strategically important at that given moment. This improves your chance of becoming more valuable and more widely recognised. You might enjoy your role more, too, as you get more closely connected to the bigger picture.

One of the most frequent complaints I hear from clients is that they feel stuck in their role. Alice's comments are typical:

> 'I have lost enthusiasm for my job. I can do the job with my eyes closed. In fact, I'm so good at my job, my boss doesn't want to promote me. It doesn't matter how hard I work. My potential is not being recognised.'

Unfortunately, Alice's comments are familiar symptoms of not approaching a career strategically. Alice had been working as a strategist in a technology company at the same level for nearly a decade. By contrast, Jessica, an operations manager for a hedge fund, was further along the discovery curve when we first met. Jessica explained:

> 'I now realise that my career was stalling because I was lost in the daily detail. This is what fuelled my career in the beginning. I was great at getting my hands dirty, jumping in and sorting out the detail. It made me feel valued as everyone knew who to come to, to get things done. Then I realised while I was busting a gut, others were contemplating where they were going to progress to next. This one change in perspective has made a massive difference to my career trajectory and job satisfaction.'

To think strategically about your future, it's crucial to approach your role in the context of a career rather than just a job. A job centres on the near term: delivery of tasks, deadlines, immediate monetary compensation and daily activities. A career, on the other hand, centres on the medium to long term: recognition, professional development and alignment of the role to strategically important topics to which you can add value. Too many of us focus solely on the job and the here and now. And we do it so well. I am not suggesting that we give up paying attention to delivering quality work and meeting deadlines. We just can't make that the be-all and end-all, as it will eventually hold us back. When we do a job so well, and for a long time, our boss isn't motivated to help us develop. Let's face it, it's hard to imagine anyone else doing our job to such perfection. The downside of course is that we lose our zest for the job because it's no longer challenging. Are you doing a job or building a career? At all levels of your career, this strategic thinking will impact your progression.

You are the business

Pursue your career as if *you* are the business. You are the best-selling brand and you understand that brand fully. You are flexible and agile at adapting yourself as external circumstances change, as any top-notch global brand would. A healthy brand is never static. The funny thing is that thinking of yourself as a business is also helping your company. It truly is a win–win. You're looking at your potential from a broader perspective. Like a business, think about your unique selling points to the company and to the industry. What are your individual *strengths* and *weaknesses* and what are the *opportunities* and *threats* in your company and industry? This analysis will clarify how you need to position yourself for growth.

This type of business analysis applied to individuals has yielded fascinating results during the career strategy workshops I run for years. Take Anna, for example. Anna worked for a global technology company and most of her experience and background was in auditing. She was frustrated that her career was stalling. One of her key obstacles was that she actually didn't like auditing. Applying business thinking to her own positioning resulted in an 'aha' moment. One of her strengths was her knowledge of local markets (which she had gained through her audit work) and her ability to suggest strategic changes to gain efficiency and results. At the same time, the UK market in which she was based was near saturation point. The opportunity for the company and the industry to expand was in fact in local markets – the smaller countries in Europe as well the Middle East and Africa. Anna uncovered the perfect match: her strength in local markets and the company's ambition to grow the business outside the UK. I always know when clients have figured out their correct alignment – between their strengths and what their companies and industry need – as their voices and body language become more animated. It's a moment to be treasured. They have rediscovered their enthusiasm for their careers.

Strategy is the foundation for stepping up

Thinking strategically goes hand in hand with career progression. Those at senior levels take time to imagine what's possible beyond the here and now. They ask why or why not. They are not absorbed in the day-to-day at the expense of having an eye on the future, which ensures the organisation is positioned for growth. Before I became Managing Director in banking, I was superb at *delivering*. That's what I was known for. I was laser-focused on the day-to-day and executing the task at hand. The firm had just introduced 360-degree performance evaluations which required feedback from peers as well as others more senior than me, from within and outside my department. It was the first time I had experienced this kind of thorough and comprehensive feedback. I'd like to tell you that it was a wonderful experience. It wasn't. It was soul-destroying. I'm sure I received many positive comments, but the ones that swirled around in my head were the negatives. This is in fact a common reaction to feedback, as our primitive brains exaggerate the negative to help us survive and be prepared for danger.

The overwhelming, consistent and clear message from nearly all my peers was that I did not make an effort to understand the bigger picture, nor try to connect and build relationships with colleagues outside of my specific department. Wow. It was like being punched in the gut – didn't others see how hard I worked? My career goal was to progress to senior management (Managing Director). Getting to that level would enable me to influence the company's culture and future direction. Once I had calmed down and allowed my rational brain to process the information, I realised the feedback was actually good. It was obvious now what I needed to do to convince others of my leadership qualities. While I still needed to deliver, I decided to be more selective about which pieces of work to focus on, keeping larger strategic issues in mind as well as seeking to gain exposure across departments. I did not need to reinvent myself but rather tweak my behaviour and realign it to address the specific issues raised in the feedback.

The pushback I hear from this approach is, 'But all the things I was doing before still need to be done.' I'd question the validity of that statement first. Is that really the case? It's important to challenge your assumptions. The environment is evolving so rapidly that checking that you're involved in the right activities should become regular practice. Second, does it make sense that *you're* the one doing that activity? Could it be a growth opportunity for someone else rather than a well-rehearsed task for you? This is a classic dilemma that many professionals face when moving from being a doer to a manager or leader. This transition is critical, however, to create the space to think and act more strategically.

Stepping outside your comfort zone

When I ask clients what they think they need to do to progress, they often cite acquisition of specific experience and professional qualifications. This may be true to some degree, but for many of us the real issue is we're not marketing ourselves. Others don't see the excellent work we do and how we add value. Getting more experience and professional qualifications is not going to fix that. Perhaps there's a bit of hiding behind the thought 'I don't have enough skills'. Be honest, are you holding back and staying in your comfort zone? The harsh truth is that you've got to take risks in order to experience the personal growth that fuels career progression.

Exactly like a business, if there's no risk, there's no return. In your career, be prepared to take risks. Remember you'll never be ready. The irony is, if you feel ready, you probably aren't setting yourself a big enough goal. And if you wait to feel ready, the opportunity is likely to have passed. Our world is evolving at a frenetic pace. Not taking a risk is the biggest risk of all.

I recently listened to a McKinsey podcast entitled 'How Companies Become Digital Leaders' and I was struck by the parallels between growth companies and the professional growth of individuals. Not acting doesn't reduce risk; the status quo can feel more comfortable, but the world will change around you. So the choice not to do anything could be the riskiest thing of all. Many professionals credit their accelerated career growth to a specific risk they took. Evelyn, an executive in the oil and gas sector maintains:

> 'It wasn't until I took on that overseas assignment in Kazakhstan (which no one wanted) that my career took off. Some of my colleagues thought I was crazy. I made sure that I had the backing and resources from the right senior colleagues to make it work. I also made sure I had the support I needed at home. It was scary but it was a career-defining moment without a doubt.'

Moving up the food chain

Look at your daily tasks through the telescope and the microscope. With the microscope, you evaluate each task in detail and in isolation. They all look important. They all look like they need to be done. With the telescope, ask which tasks are *truly* important? Which ones are clearly connected to the strategic plan of the organisation? Which ones are critical to the long-term success of the business? The key is to prioritise using these strategic lenses. If you only look through the microscope, you may find yourself executing tasks that are inconsequential. It's busy work. We are good at hiding behind busy work because we're scared of delving into tougher situations or the unknown. We're taking cover in the comfort zone. On the other hand, if you only look through the telescope, you may miss a detail that is vital to the success of a project, client problem, etc. Using both the microscope and telescope allows you to clarify your approach.

Moving up the food chain requires delegation, and there will be other tasks that won't need to be done at all once you've considered the cost versus the benefit. One of my favourite questions to ask clients in the career workshops is, 'Now that you have a plan to take your career forward, what are you going to *stop* doing?' This question stops everyone in their tracks. The workshop participants have created these amazing personal plans on how to move their career forward, but they haven't eliminated the waste. Less is more. I know you're busy. What are you busy with? Are you doing the £1 job, the £100 job, the £1,000 job or the £10,000 job?

The goal is to fill your day with the higher-value jobs.

Esther, partner and owner of a law firm, stopped the £100 job of reviewing the first drafts of her junior lawyers' documents. She now only reviews a document once a junior lawyer feels it's ready to be sent to the client. She's also developed a checklist for her junior colleagues to follow to ensure the document has met certain criteria before she casts her eyes on it. This approach has freed up time for her to develop new business – the £10,000 job. This alignment to the higher-value jobs will energise you. You won't feel dragged down by day-to-day drudgery. The company will also benefit as the *impact* you have on the business will increase. You're happier and the firm generates more money from your activities. It's a win–win.

Understand why your role exists. What issue or need is it addressing? Think about how best you can add value. The upside of a business environment in constant flux is that it also generates new opportunities. Perhaps there's a role in the organisation where you could add even more value. Perhaps it's a role that doesn't even exist yet. Suggest it. Passivity has no place in owning your career. Find the hidden problems in your department, organisation and industry, and figure out how you can help solve them. Become an expert on something valuable.

Companies are constantly rejigging their business models and shifting strategies. Company goals are a moving target. Which part of the marketplace should they be going after? What are the new technologies that should be embraced? Which client segments are now the most profitable? The list goes on. The next questions are which employees are best positioned to help us with the new strategy, and which employees are managing or even thriving in this climate of change and disruption. The employees who are constantly realigning themselves to the future are the ones who will be prioritised for promotion. It's a myth that promotions largely relate to past performance. Promotions are predominantly linked to how much an organisation values the potential contribution of an employee to its *future* direction and strategy.

Getting promoted is more complicated than it may seem, especially the more senior you become. Doing a brilliant job is the starting point rather than the overriding factor to securing a promotion. As Managing Director

I regularly participated in the annual promotion meetings to consider staff who were up for Director or Managing Director. I recall one meeting when Thomas was being put forward. One of the other Manager Directors shouted out, 'Who the f*** is Thomas? If he acts like a Director why don't I know him?' This incident reminded me that in order to get promoted you must be seen and you've got to secure the buy-in and support of the key influencers and decision makers. The steps on that career ladder become more slippery the higher you climb. You can't go it alone. The other lesson I learned is that you have to already be operating at that higher level before you're even considered ready to be promoted.

Focus on strategic outcomes

Any good manager cares about outcomes and results rather than the *how* (how you're going about achieving those desired outcomes). It's when managers don't trust us that they become over-interested in the details of *how* we're going to do it. Focusing on impact and outcomes is also the linchpin for negotiating a more flexible work schedule. As long as you start with the outcomes you're delivering, and then mention how you work at your best (working from home a certain number of days, staggered office hours, etc), your manager shouldn't care. Think like a business owner. By taking full responsibility and accountability for your deliverables, you're more likely to be granted the autonomy you desire. In my coaching conversation, the issue of needing to work flexibly often comes up. Flexibility is often required to facilitate family logistics.

My client Hilary worked in a top accounting firm for nearly twenty years. After gathering the courage to make a change, she pursued her dream of moving into industry and landed a job in the finance department of a FTSE 100 company at the first interview. There was one problem. She had not discussed office working hours and she couldn't possibly accept the job unless she was able to work flexibly. Let's be clear. She was more than happy to take on that senior role. She had no doubt she could do the job. She was prepared to make or take calls from home when the need arose or be on her laptop after she put the kids to bed. It wasn't a question of whether she could do the job.

'What am I going to do?' she shrieked in panic after the successful job interview. We talked about setting up a second meeting to show her interest in the job and demonstrate her professionalism.

The key to approaching the subject of working flexibly is to make it a non-issue. Hilary scheduled the second meeting. During that meeting she was able to ask questions about the role and share specific stories illustrating her ability to execute the job requirements. At the end of that fulsome discussion, Hilary adeptly brought up the subject of flexibility. She simply stated, 'I want to be upfront on how I work at my best.' She explained her work patterns and her commitment to her kids. How did her boss react? He wasn't bothered in the least. He acknowledged that that was a logistical concern which Hilary obviously had in hand given her impressive career history. With no need for further discussion, Hilary accepted the job offer and is thriving in her new role.

MY ACTION PLAN

1. Success for me in the next one to two years means…

2. Given my goals, the mindset and behaviours required are…

3. The ways I'm staying within my comfort zone are best described as…

4. The outcome or result that would make it worthwhile to take a risk is…

5. The specific actions I'm going to take to move out of my comfort zone and progress my career are…

References

Eblin, Scott, *Overworked and Overwhelmed: The Mindfulness Alternative*, John Wiley & Sons, 2014.

Henry, Alan and Fishbein, Rebecca, 'The Science of Breaking Out of Your Comfort Zone (and Why You Should)', 2019, https://lifehacker.com/the-science-of-breaking-out-of-your-comfort-zone-and-w-656426705 [accessed 22 November 2019].

MBASkool.com, 'Brand Promise', no date, www.mbaskool.com/business-concepts/marketing-and-strategy-terms/7506-brand-promise.html [accessed 22 November 2019].

McKinsey & Company, 'How Companies Become Digital Leaders', January 2016, https://

mckinsey.com/industries/technology-media
-and-telecommunications/our-insights/how
-companies-become-digital-leaders [accessed
12 December 2019].

Mohr, Tara Sophia, 'Why Women Don't Apply
for Jobs Unless They're 100% Qualified', *Harvard
Business Review*, 2014, https://hbr.org/2014/08
/why-women-dont-apply-for-jobs-unless-theyre
-100-qualified [accessed 22 November 2019].

Peters, Tom and Waterman Jr, Robert H, *In
Search of Excellence: Lessons from America's Best-
run Companies*, 2nd edition, Profile Books, 2004.

The Economist, 'SWOT analysis', 2009, https://
economist.com/news/2009/11/11/swot-analysis
[accessed 22 November 2019].

Thomson, Peninah, *The Rise of the Female
Executive: How Women's Leadership Is Accelerating
Cultural Change*, Palgrave Macmillan, 2015.

Crack The Confidence Code

Have you ever felt that your confidence levels are holding you back from getting that bigger role, plum promotion, or higher pay? Have you ever wondered how others manage to look confident, even in the most challenging and stressful situations? (It's so annoying, isn't it?) How do they do it and what is this mysterious confidence code? The link between confidence and career progression is widely documented, especially pertaining to female professionals. Why is it so important? In a business environment that is in a constant state of flux, being confident taking on something new is crucial, no matter what your profession, industry or sector. Today the only constant is in fact change itself. Learning how to deal with change increases our confidence. We're not thrown off course because something isn't like it used to be. Our confidence grows when we embrace change and see it as an opportunity for personal and professional development.

We live in a new normal

Before we jump into tactics for increasing your confidence, it's worth taking a moment to observe what's happening around us that could be causing us to feel unsettled and less confident. The world of work for companies and employees has shifted to a new normal. It's a phenomenon witnessed across every industry around the globe. What exactly is going on?

Every organisation is being disrupted by technology. Technology has *accelerated* the pace of globalisation. It has enabled flexible working and led to the viability of virtual working and teams. Technology has also made business more complex and increased competition. Linked to technology is the *over-abundance* of data. Companies are swimming in it. The sheer amount of information and data is multiplying at an accelerated rate. Companies are dealing with 24–7 client demands as a result of technology and globalisation. Company reorganisations and restructurings are no longer one-offs or extraordinary events – they have become part of the status quo. The external market is also changing at an ever-increasing pace. Internally, even if the organisation isn't changing at the top level, you may be experiencing an adjusted reporting line, an additional manager (matrix reporting), or a new team. Jobs for life are ancient history and there is no longer stigma attached to moving companies. With everyone living longer, there's an expectation that we will be switching organisations and careers multiple times during our professional lives.

While organisations are undergoing change, individuals are also feeling the direct pain of 24–7 accessibility and are expected to do the same amount of work with smaller teams. They are trying to cope with meeting and email overload, increased competition (from machines and the global workforce) and complex reporting structures. There is pressure to consume, process and manage enormous amounts of information. Nearly all my clients report that – especially since the 2008 financial crisis – there is more and more information being circulated that needs to be absorbed and managed, often resulting in a sense of overwhelm. And while virtual working can be a godsend for work–life balance, it can also present challenges in terms of diminished visibility, work discipline and sense of belonging to a team. The way we forge career paths is also evolving. There's a redefinition of what a 'successful' career path looks like. Traditional career paths can be viewed as a straight line of progression, centred on title, money and power. Non-linear career paths are windy and generally built around personal fulfilment, professional growth, autonomy and a broad definition of remuneration.

As a baby boomer, I recognise this revised picture of how we think about careers. When I graduated from university, the focus was on feeding myself, ie money. My path was more or less a straight line. I observe with my adult kids that for them, it's about personal fulfilment and autonomy. My son joined one of the large accounting firms right after university. With a few years' experience under his belt, he observed, 'Mum, I don't get this hierarchy thing. What's the point?' I realised then a generational shift had occurred. Meanwhile, alongside these macro and micro business changes, our personal lives continue to evolve: changing family situations (life partners, kids, elderly parents), new-found personal interests, and health challenges. We are busy people coping with enormous amounts of change at home and at work. This is our new normal.

Strive for confidence and competence in equal measure

Why is confidence so important? Confidence is *directly linked* to career progression. Career progression is about competence and confidence in equal measure. The more confident you are, the more likely you are to reach your career goals. It's generally not about one big action that you didn't take, but rather scores of smaller actions and situations where you hesitated to put yourself forward. Small actions lead to big progress. Many of us know at some level that it's necessary to be adaptable to change, but we don't feel confident to take certain risks. What's standing in our way? It's the big F-word: fear. The good news here is it's your *choice*: you can choose to be paralysed by fear and let it hold you back or you can choose to take a deep breath, face the fear and take action in spite of it. I'm not suggesting that you pretend you're not fearful. Accept the fear. Some are better at hiding it than others. Acknowledge it, but don't let it consume you. Remember it's *your choice* on how you respond. Choosing to do nothing is a choice. Do you really want to give control over your career, your future to someone else? Non-action is abdicating control to others.

On the whole topic of fear, I firmly believe it's first and foremost about *courage* rather than confidence. It's having the courage to take the leap into the unknown and the unfamiliar. Courage is the quality of mind or spirit that enables a person to face difficulty, danger and pain. Interestingly, the root of the word courage is *cor*, the Latin word for 'heart' (related to the French word *coeur*). It's less about logic and the mind and more about the heart, and a brave heart at that. If you've ever watched a professional tennis tournament, you'll have noticed many of the players pound their fists against their heart when they've made a courageous shot.

Tap into your courage memory bank

Remembering the times when you did have the courage to do new and scary things will give you the confidence to do the same again.

It's an upward spiral. Rita's family moved from England to France when she was a teenager – a tough move at that age. She felt a tremendous amount of peer pressure as the outlier. She was the English kid, not born and raised in France. When it came to studying for her baccalaureate, she encountered utter discouragement and disbelief from her fellow students as well as her teachers. They mocked her attempt to succeed at the baccalaureate, especially in French literature. Rita got the last laugh. She achieved not only the highest result in her class, but one of the top scores in all of France for French literature. How about that for underestimating someone's potential?

Rita now works for a management consulting firm in London. When I met Rita, she was looking for support to secure a promotion. She absolutely deserved the promotion based on her performance, but as we've discussed, performance is only going to get you so far. In order to secure the promotion, Rita had to face her fear of networking and 'put herself out there' to improve her visibility with senior management. They needed to see her exceptional ability and her ambition to step up to the next level.

'I am fundamentally a shy person. How can I move forward?' inquired Rita.

Aware of her experience as a teenager, I reminded her of her unbelievable courage as a student in France. 'Courage comes from the same place,' I said. 'It doesn't matter if that courageous action was in your personal or professional life.'

Recalling her time in France gave Rita the courage to interact with senior management and talk about how she was adding value. That surely must have been easier than getting the top score in French literature in all of France. Rita continued to make a conscious effort to be visible to her managers and they awarded her the promotion.

Curb the confidence killers

Curb the three main confidence killers. These are:

1. Playing it too safe

2. Overthinking

3. Striving for perfection

Each of these undermines confidence. Worse yet, if you get tripped up by one of these, it can easily lead to a downward spiral. When your confidence is increasing, it can feel like it's increasing exponentially. One positive experience builds on the next. Conversely, when your confidence is decreasing, it can feel like a downward spiral that's out of control.

Playing it too safe is dangerous

I'm not encouraging reckless behaviour when I say don't play it too safe. I'm not suggesting throwing caution to the wind. I am saying, however, that without taking risks, the rewards are minimal. Additionally, playing it too safe in an environment of rapid change can be the riskiest strategy of all. It's the start of that slippery slope in terms of your career. Too safe means you can do your job in your sleep. There is no challenge left. You are no longer motivated to put in the effort. You feel unfilled. You're lethargic and uninspired. It's not a positive trajectory.

Overthinking

We can talk ourselves out of anything. We are all guilty of this. The little voice in our head comes up with all sorts of creative reasons why we can't push ourselves. We are phenomenal at this. We are also adept at exaggerating the most innocuous criticism in our own head. (Our primitive brains do this to protect us from danger.) My client Clarissa, a geologist for a multinational company, shared that seven years earlier a colleague had criticised her for networking with senior colleagues. He had told her she was too political. She had taken this criticism quite hard. The truth was that many members of the senior management team were also from Latin America, like Clarissa, so they had a lot of shared life experience.

Clarissa obsessed over her colleague's negative comment. She overthought things and let it stop her from taking career-enhancing actions. She became reluctant to speak up and continue to build her network. She retreated from net-working and became inwardly fixed on her day job. She dramatically changed her behaviour for the subsequent seven years, to the detriment of her career. She lost connection to the 'hot' projects or topics. Senior management was no longer aware of her progress and what she was involved in. Upon reflection, Clarissa realises she let that one comment derail her, a comment that was likely motivated by jealousy rather than intent to help.

Striving for perfection is a losing game

By definition, the new thing that you're going to learn and take on board to stretch yourself, you will not be able to execute to perfection. Be patient with yourself. Cut yourself some slack. Don't set the bar too high – you're still a learner. Striving for perfection is a game you'll never win. It can paralyse you as a result. Your confidence will be knocked, and then you'll be even less confident, unable to take any further risks. You're certainly starting in the right place for career progression when you set yourself ambitious goals. These will remain aspirational, however, unless you take the plunge and take action to fulfil them. Enough planning. Take the step into unchartered waters. You've got to be willing to accept imperfection and not let it hold you back. This is where many promising careers can get derailed.

Taking imperfect action is a game-changer

Getting something done at say 70% or 80% is better than the procrastinator who waits to take any action because she doesn't believe she can achieve perfection. Begin living and working with the mindset that you will never get it 100% right. I also find that when I'm working on a piece of work such as a proposal or report, it's better to get it say 80% right and then ask for feedback. Feedback is the way to quickly and significantly improve the quality of work. If I've poured my heart and soul into a draft and think it's perfect, I'm less open to feedback. In that context, I'm likely to defend my work and resist any amendments or suggestions for improvement.

The other factor to take into consideration is the level of perfection warranted by the task at hand. In some instances, a high level of perfection will be required because lives are at stake. In a business context, where there are tight deadlines and shifting priorities, if you wait until you've achieved a 100%, the value of that work could drop to zero. Yes, zero. Why? The situation has moved on and that information is no longer needed or relevant. Perhaps a new strategy has now been adopted. Or worse yet, someone else put forward a proposal (almost identical to yours) and the company is running with that. Your ideas and your work now appear stale. In business, there is always a trade-off between time and perfection. Instead of striving for perfection, determine what the appropriate trade-off is for that specific circumstance.

Potential side effects of perfectionism

Perfectionists may also encounter damaging side effects: incredibly demanding on self, high expectations on self, negative behaviour, lack of presence or gravitas, and overwhelm and stress. When you're so demanding on yourself it impacts confidence. You're preoccupied with what you *haven't* accomplished rather than what you *have*. You're fixated on what didn't go well rather than what did go well. The natural inclination is to exaggerate the negative and discount the positive.

When we set the bar too high, it becomes problematic to delegate. This is what I refer to as the 'Superwoman Syndrome' that I suffered at the beginning of my career. I felt like I had to do everything because others couldn't do it as well as I could. The result is you turn into a control freak and micromanager. As a professional you are unable to develop and coach others as you're not giving them the space to learn and develop. This behaviour crushes leadership potential. It's not a confidence builder, but rather a massive energy drainer and you eventually burn out. You become sensitive about any comments about your work. Any comments you take as criticism rather than seizing the opportunity to learn how you could improve. You become impatient with others and cynical. You are less likely to be collaborative and open. Nobody likes a perfectionist.

Getting caught in the weeds was one of the reasons my career wasn't progressing to that senior level. As mentioned earlier, my performance reports indicated that I wasn't 'strategic' enough. That's generally a code word for a good doer rather than leader or manager. Select carefully the types of activities you get involved in and associate yourself with. You can make yourself look more junior by taking on the less significant, less strategic tasks. When you're caught in the minutiae, you're also likely not to have the time to look up and see the bigger picture. You've boxed yourself into a position where it's not possible for you think strategically. Achieving perfection was never possible, and it's even less so in the new normal environment that we live in. The world is complex and perpetually evolving. Nothing can be 100% controlled – there are too many moving parts.

My client Lauren was entangled in this perfectionist juggernaut. She worked as a lawyer for one of the top law firms in London, the so-called 'magic circle'. Only the best graduates get offers from firms within this circle. Lauren was first rate. She contacted me soon after she had been told that her name had been excluded from the partner promotion list. She was utterly devastated. How could that possibly be? She had worked unbelievably hard. She had given it her all and sacrificed so much of her personal time. My first question to her was which partners had she lobbied to support her promotion to partner? I received a blank stare. She then countered, 'Christine, why does that matter. I have a stellar reputation in the office. There's even a thing called the "Lauren job". When colleagues come to me for help, they expect a level of detail and perfection they are in awe of.' She then recounted a situation where a colleague advised that a certain piece of work didn't need a 'Lauren job'. That confused her.

'What do you mean? Of course, I'm going to give it my absolute best.'

In order to meet the usual tight deadlines, Lauren often worked through the night. While Lauren was digging into a level of detail that her colleagues could only dream of, her colleagues were out and about chatting with partners about the future strategy of the firm, how they could add value, how ready they were for the promotion, etc. What Lauren only discovered in hindsight was that not all pieces of work deserve the gold standard level of attention. The other lesson learned was that unless others know about your ambition and your ability to deliver gold standard work, the true value of that work gets overlooked. On a positive note, Lauren now works for a securities regulator and loves it. She is a changed woman. She makes a point to go out to lunch with a new colleague every week. She's in the loop about how much attention to give to which legal cases. No more head down without understanding the wider environment. My friend and client Marie, a senior risk manager in one of the large accounting firms, goes a step further in her advice: 'You should never do a job perfectly. At all levels you should be dedicating a certain amount of time to creating options for your next step. Be clear on the impact you want to make in your current role as well as having an eye on your next role.'

Career breaks build confidence

I have worked with many women over the years who have returned from maternity leave and felt that their confidence has been hurt. This is understandable. There is, however, an alternative story. Career breaks can also be an ideal opportunity to *build* your confidence. Just back from maternity leave, Francesca clarified, 'My career break instilled in me the *confidence* to try new things without worrying about the outcome.' This was after Francesca's first child. She realised that whatever issue her child had, she was going to sort it out – 'no ifs, ands or buts.' Francesca works as a seasoned co-ordinator for international cultural exchanges. Before her leave, Francesca fretted over every minor detail. After having spent many sleepless nights caring for a sick child, Francesca's perspective on life was transformed. The problems and challenges at work didn't seem that trying anymore. They certainly weren't life-threatening. Francesca returned to work as a more mature and confident professional, displaying an openness to solving problems in a calm and reassuring fashion. Her leave elevated her career.

Anne, an executive in the hospitality industry, had a similar experience. Now back from leave, Anne is less worried about what others might think. She also feels she's able to step back and look at the bigger picture, which has increased the value of her work. Anne claims, 'Stepping out of the career gave me insight into myself, and more trust in myself.' The point is that any kind of break – whether it be maternity, medical leave, a sabbatical or leave to care for an elderly parent – can boost your confidence and therefore be career-enhancing. Consider how your break – even shorter breaks like holidays and weekends – contributes to your performance at work through improved motivation, concentration, fresh insight, and sharpened interpersonal skills. This past summer, my husband and I cycled from Rotterdam to Vienna – 1,400 miles in total, self-guided, and with our personal belongings packed in the panniers on the bikes. It was an amazing trip, working as a team, taking each day at a time and dipping into the local cultures. We cycled on average sixty miles a day. The longest daily ride was seventy-five miles. After four weeks literally on the road, I returned home with a renewed sense of confidence. The cycling trip was a positive rather than a negative for my career. I returned to work with my battery fully recharged and able to be at my best for my clients.

MY ACTION PLAN

1. I want to be more confident in…
2. The areas I am most fearful of are…
3. The motivation I need to get over this fear is…
4. The memory which can help me build confidence is…
5. The two or three main imperfect actions I'm committed to take in order to develop myself further are…

References

Brown, Brené, *Daring Greatly: How the Courage to Be Vulnerable Transforms the Way We Live, Love, Parent and Lead*, Penguin Life, 2015.

Dweck, Carol S, *Mindset: How You Can Fulfil Your Potential*, Robinson, 2012.

Kay, Katty and Shipman, Claire, *The Confidence Code*, HarperCollins, 2014.

Kübler-Ross, Elisabeth, *On Death and Dying*, Macmillan, 1969.

Peer, Marisa, *I Am Enough: Mark Your Mirror and Change Your Life*, Marisa Peer, 2018.

Prime Your Personal Brand

Like successful consumer products, others can't know how good you are unless they know you and what you stand for – your brand. By building your brand, you increase your prospects for personal growth, professional advancement and a successful career path. Without a brand our talent, innovative ideas and drive for excellence literally sit on the shelf. We don't stand out. Others don't even see us to select us. Where are you on the brand spectrum? Are you clear on what your brand is? If yes, do others recognise that brand and understand what your brand stands for? Do you know how others perceive you? Do they know you and what you bring to the table? Creating a clear and compelling brand underpins our ability to be seen, heard and recognised. Recognition is integral to keeping us motivated. It's not a 'nice-to-have' but a driving force in maintaining our momentum and enthusiasm to achieve our goals.

Your brand permeates your personal business plan

When reflecting on your personal business plan (as *you* are the business), be sure to link each of the elements back to your brand. Like a business, the key elements of your personal plan include strategy, products and services, clients, capital expenditure (capex), marketing and risk management. Jessica, the operations manager I mentioned in chapter one who has emerged from the minutiae, has worked hard priming her brand and developing her personal business plan. Her strategy is to become an Operations Director. Previously, she worked at a larger fund that invested in technology, processes and procedures to handle large volumes of trading. Jessica's new employer has been expanding non-stop for the last five years, constantly creating one-off processes to handle the new trades. This is both the opportunity and the challenge for Jessica. The infrastructure is not robust enough to support higher levels of growth, yet the fund continues to increase trading volumes. Breakdowns have become a daily occurrence. Jessica accepted this new role as it aligned to her strategy of wanting to 'own something'.

Her ambition is to transform the infrastructure (technology, processes and procedures) as well as the culture to support the firm's ambitious growth targets. Her products and services encompass the management and transformation of the department. Her client base consists of her boss (head of operations and product control), the heads of trading, the chief financial officer, the chief administrative officer and the CEO. Jessica is a firm believer in investing in her career. Her capex investments include her annual gym membership, one-on-one coaching and building relationships with her team as well as her 'clients'. Jessica's brand can be described as no-nonsense, effective and transformational. Jessica realises that not rocking the boat is perhaps the safe or less risky option, but that's not who she is. She believes that she was hired to shake things up and that's exactly what she's doing.

Build your brand using the CODE formula

Now that you have a deeper understanding of how your personal brand fits into your overall career strategy, let's dig into how to build your brand in practice. The formula for building a successful brand is CODE:

- **C**apture the key aspects of your brand

- **O**kay your brand with others

- **D**evelop *and deliver* your brand

- **E**valuate your brand continuously

C – Capture the key aspects of your brand

Capture the key features of your brand by asking yourself the big questions: Who am I? What do I want people to say about me around the coffee machine? What really matters to me? What gets me out of bed in the morning? Where do I get my energy from?

First, reflect on your skills, hard as well as soft skills. You could be a great listener, team builder or problem-solver in addition to exemplifying first rate financial or technical skills as well as deep industry knowledge. Second, incorporate your interests, personal as well as professional. In your personal life you may be a keen runner, have a family or be a volunteer for local community project. In your professional life, a certain market segment, technical area or emerging industry trend may be appealing to you. Third, integrate your values into your brand. Your values might be honesty, openness or a strong work ethic, to name a few. Fourth, include your personal qualities such as thoughtfulness, patience, exacting standards, etc. Fifth, add your personal and professional experiences. Experiences make us who we are. Experiences in our personal life can give us clues as to why we behave in a certain way. View yourself as the *whole* you.

Lastly, bring in your goals and aspirations. Your brand is a promise that you will perform in the future in a certain area. It sends a signal to others about the direction in which you want to head. Your brand is not self-serving. We are helping others to know how to place us and how best to leverage our skills and talents. A symptom that our brand needs updating is when we get pegged for a certain position or task which is below our goals, aspirations and potential. If others only see us as the 'doer', we get labelled as the doer and never get invited to the senior management party where our input and ideas would be better served. So often we define our brand narrowly as skills and experiences. A brand is so much more than that. Simply continuing to build our skills and professional experience does not lead to an improved brand. It's the values, aspirations, personal qualities and personal experiences that prepare us for leadership.

O – Okay your brand with others

What might be missing in your brand? Okay it with others. In other words, validate your thoughts by asking for feedback. Friends and family are a good place to start as they are friendly faces. They are also helpful as we often show another side of ourselves to them that we may not share or be as open about at work. Friends and family tend to know what makes us happy and what we really care about – sometimes more than we realise. Effective leadership and inspiring others require us to tap into our personal beliefs and values. It's who we really are. Friends and family can hold up that mirror to help us see ourselves more clearly. Also seek feedback from colleagues, bosses, clients and mentors. Feedback from this broad set of individuals provides the full range of perspectives on our various roles and behaviours. Here are some suggestions for questions to ask: What are your current perceptions of me? How would you best describe me? What are my strengths and weaknesses? What should be my priority areas to expand or improve?

Throughout my corporate career, I have found it incredibly useful to chat with others to understand how I was perceived or how I came across. Make no mistake about it – it's scary. If you approach this with an open mind and an open heart, others will respond positively. Showing your vulnerability makes you likeable. It makes you human. What surprised me the most when I solicited this kind of personal feedback was that I was much harder on myself than others were. For instance, I learned that although I had a reputation for being demanding, others liked working with me and for me because I was optimistic and fun to work with. I recognised the demanding characteristic but was completely surprised by the 'optimistic and fun' comments.

Working in tough competitive environments, you need to build alliances. A word of caution is warranted here. Only solicit feedback from those you *trust*. This is sensitive information and in the hands of a rogue character, such information could be used to hurt you. A rogue character will exploit newly discovered information about your personal insecurities and so-called 'weaknesses' by spreading vicious gossip intended to undermine you.

D – Develop and deliver your brand

What is the content of your message and how will you deliver it? When thinking about your key message, imagine you're in a lift and you only have a few minutes to introduce yourself. What's your pitch? The pitch should be short and sweet and delivered with infectious enthusiasm. If you're not enthusiastic and positive about your elevator pitch, do you think others will be inclined to listen? For those who already know you, storytelling is an effective tactic for reinforcing the messages about your brand. A message encapsulated within a story increases the chances of the story being repeated, and in some circumstances even going viral. In a business environment where there is so much dry, impersonal information, communicating via stories makes you stand out as you're connecting with your audience on an emotional level.

As with any good marketing plan, be clear on *whom* you are targeting. Given your career strategy, who are the people who need to know you, like you and trust you? To clarify, to like you doesn't mean others have to agree with you. We can like others who hold opposite opinions, as long as they are honest and truthful. By contrast, it's hard to like people who appear to be acting or insincere. Given where you are looking to go next, who are the notable individuals who need to be familiar with your brand? Your audience could be individuals outside of your immediate department, so that you can get access to a wider set of opportunities. If you're focusing on getting your brand better known on a project you are working on, your audience could include the stakeholders associated with that project. Being specific about the audience will help you tailor your message appropriately. It's useful to customise your core brand in certain circumstances. For example, perhaps you're in the middle of a horrific project and you need to protect your reputation against negative backlash. Your personal brand can be part of an offensive as well as defensive strategy here. In this tricky situation, it would be important to highlight the aspects of the project that are going well and how you've been successful in managing the risks.

In delivering your brand, bear in mind how you want to be portrayed in all settings: in person, on the telephone or video calls, and in writing (emails, proposals and reports as well as social media). Your brand should be consistently portrayed across all these modes of communication. Your 'in person' brand covers a gamut of interactions: team meetings, project catch-ups, one-on-ones, company social events and charity functions, among others. Jessica (the operations manager) was debating what to wear at the hedge fund's end-of-year black-tie dinner. Jessica doesn't leave details to chance. She asked me if I'd mind reviewing a couple of photos of dresses she was contemplating wearing. I was flattered that she valued my opinion. I was also impressed by how thoughtful she was about the brand she was portraying. Given that Jessica's objective was to advance to Operations Director, the choice was easy – definitely the more elegant black dress fit the part. The dress revealed femininity, intelligence and authority all at the same time, reflecting Jessica herself.

E – Evaluate your brand continuously

Once you have identified and built your brand, remember to continue strengthening and protecting it and re-evaluating it in line with your current strategic objectives. It's a continuous loop. Your brand needs to stay fresh. Your brand is a living thing – it's dynamic. There will always be competing brands (jobseekers) ready to fill any gap you leave behind. You are indeed founder and CEO of You Ltd, and the more you do to cultivate your personal brand, the more successful you will be in your current role as well as your future positions.

Solicit ongoing feedback. It's not a one-off process. It's constant. Refresh the assessors you solicit feedback from. As you become more experienced, you'll change, your brand will need updating and therefore the people who you're asking for feedback may need updating as well. Incorporate new experience and successes. This applies across the board in the branding process. Considering recently achieved experiences and success, you'll want to refresh and tweak your brand message and the stories you tell. Keep the stories fresh. This will help you maintain your enthusiasm, too. You're likely to get bored repeatedly telling the same stories. You'll also want to think about how to align those new experiences and successes to your latest goal.

You may also want to take into consideration any 'failures' you may have had. Failure, by the way, is only failure when we don't learn from that experience. What have you learned? How has that made you better? How has it made you more seasoned and able to handle the future better? How has this made you a better professional? Update your brand in respect of these 'failures'. You're not the same person you were before. Experience – good and bad – is worth something.

Strengthen your brand through consistency

Strong personal brands, like consumer brands, are consistent in what they stand for. Although a brand may be tweaked and refined to take into consideration a specific target audience, the core message doesn't change significantly. A confused brand leads to poor reputations. Trust requires consistency. With a consistent brand, others know what to expect. There are no nasty surprises. Consistency also ensures that your brand is the same regardless of whether it pertains to your personal or professional life. It's the same you, so it's the same brand.

A few years ago, a good friend based in the US introduced us to another American family who had just moved to the UK. Ester and Daniel had two young boys. I contacted Ester to organise lunch at our home so our families could meet up. The week leading up to the lunch had been a normal busy week for my other half, Tom. That Friday evening, he was asked to join a conference call with about ten other professionals (bankers, lawyers, accountants and company executives) to discuss what assurances the accountants could make on the financial information in the prospectus for the company's bond offering. Tom, a partner at one of the top accounting firms, had moved departments and was technically no longer involved in transactions. Nevertheless, the law firm involved in the bond transaction asked for Tom by name to join the call. Tom's brand was consistent. He had developed a reputation for working with the various stakeholders involved in bond offerings in a collaborative, yet firm and professional way.

I could end the story there – it's a fantastic example of what a brand does for you. You're a hero before you've even entered the room. But there's more. The call was testy, with the bankers and lawyers demanding that the accountants make assurances for *all* the financial information. Tom, accustomed to being under fire, talked through the logic of why his accounting firm could give assurances on some numbers but not others. The accountants couldn't give assurances about forecasts, but only on numbers that they had audited. The lawyer from one of the main banks funding the deal found Tom's summary fair and reasonable. The call ended and everyone was happy to get on with weekend.

On Saturday afternoon, our guests Ester, Daniel and their boys arrived for lunch.

Tom opened the door. 'Hi, I'm Tom Quinn.'

Daniel responded bewildered, 'Tom Quinn, the accountant? Hi, I'm Daniel, the lawyer from bank ABC. I believe we met yesterday evening on a conference call?'

Both Daniel and Tom were involved in tough business negotiations the day before, but neither had let down their brands. Both were civil, professional, but assertive.

Tom continued, 'Daniel, I was fair and reasonable, right?'

'Yes, you certainly were, and I now understand why our external counsel had asked for you by name to join the call,' said Daniel.

You never know when your professional and personal life will cross – best to stay consistent.

Enjoy the benefits of promoting your brand

'Hard work speaks for itself' is the belief I held onto tightly as I joined the workforce after university. I was the polite, nice young woman who thought my good work spoke for itself. Isn't that what our parents told us? 'Work hard and you'll succeed.' This myth was luckily shattered in my mid-twenties. At that time, I had asked one of the senior consultants in the firm I was working for to write me a recommendation for applying to an MBA programme.

Hugh arranged a meeting with me in his huge office to talk about the recommendation he had written. My throat was in my stomach. I was so worried and ill at ease.

'Christine, I've written you a commendable recommendation. This should certainly help you get into the MBA programme you're hoping for. Let's just put that to the side for now. The reason I wanted to meet up with you is to give you feedback on your working style. You are far too quiet. Many people in the organisation don't see the great work that you do and that's not good for you and that's not good for our company.'

I was stunned. My kids do not believe this story. Mum, quiet? Mum, shy? No way. Since that day, I make a conscious effort to come out my shell, not just for me, but for the benefit of those around me.

Janet is an IT manager for a global bank. She is a technologist who has learned the importance of managing relationships. She credits her success not to her exceptional technology skills but rather her ability to forge strong relationships across organisations. Janet decided last year that each of her team members should be more proactive in communicating with their stakeholders. Communication would include status updates on their various projects, expectation management and feedback on ideas and suggestions.

During a team meeting, Janet announced to her direct reports that approximately 20% of their time should be spent on stakeholder management. Shock and horror filled the meeting room. Her direct reports were deep subject experts. Social interaction was not their preferred way of working. At year end, with Janet's constant encouragement, all her direct reports had met their new objective. The productivity of the team, from the team's perspective, was on par with the prior year. The performance ratings from the businesses they supported, however, were substantially improved. In addition to tangible business results, the stakeholders felt they knew the IT team much better, understood precisely what they were working on and felt involved in the major decisions. The IT team's brand had become more visible, resulting in an increased level of trust.

Be ready to showcase your brand at any time

You never know when an opportunity is going to present itself to showcase your brand – it could be in the hallway, next to the coffee machine or during a fire drill when you find yourself next to a senior person with whom your path would not normally cross. I remember the day my banking boss, Mazz, was running by my desk.

'Christine, do you have a quick minute. I'm going up to the CEO's office and I'd like you to join me to talk about the client conference you organised.'

Mazz had a special relationship with the CEO as the CEO was from the same part of Switzerland as his stepmother. He had visited that part of Switzerland many times, so the CEO and he had a shared personal experience. I knew this was my chance. I had to let the CEO know what I did and how I'd made the conference a success.

'Here's my chance. Deep breath.' I gave myself a little pep talk in the lift on the way to the C-suite. Put on the spot, I talked about the incredibly positive feedback we had received from the investors at the conference, and the business that followed as a direct result of the event. Notice how I used the social proof of the clients to demonstrate how successful the conference was. Be ready at any moment to seize the opportunity to tell others what you're doing and how it's making an impact. In this way, others will know how to use you to help drive the organisation forward and new career-enhancing prospects will come your way.

MY ACTION PLAN

My brand consists of the six areas below. (Hint: Think about what really matters to you. What energises you? What do you want others to say about you?)

1. My skills are...
2. My interests are...
3. My values are...
4. My personal qualities are...
5. My key experiences are...
6. My goals and aspirations are...
7. I can improve the visibility of my brand by taking the following action...

References

Alba, Jason, 'Building Your Brand: Tactics for Successful Career Branding', *LiveCareer.com*, no date, https://livecareer.com/resources /careers/planning/career-branding [accessed 22 November 2019].

Cialdini, Robert B, *Influence: The Psychology of Persuasion*, revised edition, Harper Business, 2007.

Klaus, Peggy, *The Hard Truth about Soft Skills: Workplace Lessons Smart People Wish They'd Learned Sooner*, Collins, 2008.

Orji, Nneka, 'Me, Myself and I: Closing the Gap Between Perception and Reality', *TheGlassHammer.com*, no date, https:// theglasshammer.com/2017/02/01/closing-gap -perception-reality [accessed 22 November 2019].

Wyeth, Sharón Lynn, 'Your Name is Your Brand', *SelfGrowth.com*, no date, https://selfgrowth.com /articles/your-name-is-your-brand [accessed 22 November 2019].

RULE #4

Nourish Your Network

Even in today's digital age, most job offers are the result of networking rather than job adverts. If you're waiting for that ideal role to be advertised, you've already put yourself in a disadvantageous position. Others have already been making the connections, shaping the role and pitching for the job before you've even put in your application. To get ahead of the game requires one key skill – networking. The reality is that the benefits of networking go far beyond finding a job. Networking also makes you more valuable in the job as you have a broader and more strategic view of your surroundings. For many of us, one of the biggest obstacles to networking is getting over that sticky, yucky feeling when you're in an unfamiliar setting and are forced to navigate a conversation that includes talking about yourself.

Career success depends on your ability to network

You're busy. I get that. You may be thinking, 'Does networking really matter? Is it crucial to my career advancement? Can't I just do the job?' A career is like a three-legged stool. It's comprised of skills and experience, yes, but that's only two legs. Without the third leg – relationships – your career lacks a stable base to grow. Through *networking* you gain access to one of the most valuable assets in your career: other people. I empathise with the pressures of the daily grind – it's not easy to stay on top of the daily pressures. However, concentrating on merely the immediate tasks of your job, without networking and building relationships, stunts career growth. It's the lack of strong relation-ships that often trips up the most promising careers, especially the more senior you become.

The value you bring to an organisation is not simply the tasks you undertake and deliver. Your value is also determined by your *social capital.* What you bring to any organisation is not just your skills and experience, but also your current network of relationships (internal as well as external), along with your ability to forge critical relationships in the future. In my younger years, I thought I wasn't a good foot solider if I had external contacts and knew what the competition was doing. I then realised that people more senior than me were expected to know the competition from a strategic stand-point, and also with an eye to make new hires. Senior professionals are *expected* to have contacts in their industry to share non-confidential knowledge about trends and industry-related topics. Managers are expected to bring talented individuals into the company. By only knowing your own organisation, you look small-minded and junior.

Pauline was looking to switch jobs, having worked for the same technology company for the past twenty years. She was tired of the constant restructurings and was finding it difficult to maintain her motivation. I encouraged Pauline to identify respected individuals in her network, including former bosses and colleagues who had moved onto other compa-nies, whom she might get in touch with. One individual came to mind immediately – Joseph.

Pauline had worked with Joseph for seventeen years. Several years ago, Joseph had transitioned to a competitor and was now VP of Sales for Europe.

'Perfect!' I exclaimed. 'He's exactly the type of person you want to be chatting with.'

Pauline was reluctant to contact Joseph. She pushed back, 'I don't like calling in favours.'

It wasn't until I cited the statistics behind finding a new job through networking that Pauline gathered the courage to contact Joseph to set up a coffee. During their catch-up, Pauline shared that she was ready to leave the company in search for a role which would be more senior and for an organisation that would value her as an individual contributor rather than a pure line manager. Joseph was thrilled that he and Pauline had reconnected and he immediately referred Pauline to several of his colleagues for interviews.

'Pauline,' I explained, 'Here's how it works. Joseph is expected to bring in talented professionals, given his seniority. You make him look good. It's a two-way street. You are helping him as much as he's helping you.' To make sure

Pauline was fully bought into this perspective I added, 'You've invested seventeen years in this relationship. You are not cheating by being fast-tracked for an interview. You've earned it!'

Last week, Pauline accepted what she considered the ideal job offer from Joseph's company.

Set an objective for your networking strategy

Set an objective for your networking strategy so that you can extract the most value from your efforts. For example, you may want to increase your profile internally and externally. Enhancing your external profile can also be an effective way to increase your internal profile. If no one knows who you are and the top-quality work you do, the value of your work declines. Alternatively, you may want to gain a deeper insight into your organisation and your industry, which could provide the roadmap on how to align your career to future growth. Having a broader view may bolster your confidence to engage in conversations with senior leaders. Another objective could be benchmarking your current role or a potential role to ascertain your worth in the market. (Senior professionals are expected to do this – if you don't do it, you look unseasoned.) Given your level of experience and the value that you bring to an organisation, are your salary, other benefits and title in line with the sector at large? The more you value yourself, the more others will value you.

You may be looking to use networking to identify potential new hires. When you refer good people into your organisation, you're increasing your own value. You help the organisation save costs that would otherwise be paid to headhunters. Given your referral, the new hire is likely to be a better fit for the organisation as he or she has been vetted by you. You look well-connected and your social capital goes up. Finding a mentor is also an admirable goal for networking. Every successful person has had others offer them insightful advice, protected them, or opened a door for them. No sense in spinning your wheels on challenges that others before you have figured out how to navigate. Be clear on what you'd like to gain from a mentor, then pinpoint who would be best suited to meet your specific needs.

Pauline's objective was identifying new job opportunities. A deep level of trust already existed between her and her former colleague

Joseph, so it felt natural for Pauline to immediately chat about her current job and plans for the future. One common mistake in networking as a jobseeker is to immediately jump to asking for a job before building a rapport and investing in a relationship. I recall a university alumni event where I spoke on a career panel and shortly after was approached by a young alumna, Becky. I had never met Becky before. She proceeded to tell me that she found networking useless in her job search. She had sent LinkedIn messages to many alumni asking them for a job, but no one had been forthcoming.

'Becky, this doesn't surprise me,' I replied. 'You might want to tweak your approach. Perhaps your first message could be that you'd like to connect to learn more about them and their career. Is there something in their profile that fascinates you? Mention that. It's like dating – it's a process, not just one encounter.'

I experienced an 'aha' moment early on in my career, when I sheepishly asked Sam, a senior colleague at the firm I was working for, if he might know anyone in the UK as I was moving there in several months' time. I dared not walk into his office. I stood at the door, shaking (at least on the inside). Sam wasn't just any colleague. He was the son of the owner of the firm. He was extremely well-connected because of his dad, but also because he made a point to network and invest in relationships and clearly enjoyed it. Sam could see the anguish on my face and hear the trepidation in my voice.

In all his charm and warmth, Sam replied, 'Christine, come in and have a seat in my office. Let me tell you how this works. You're a smart and hard-working individual. By me connecting you with others in my network, you make me look good.' I couldn't believe what I was hearing. This turned my whole perspective on networking on its head. I am a converted networker and have never looked back. I used to dread it, but networking is now one of my favourite activities. In the end, Sam did in fact connect me with one of the other senior consultants in the firm, who unbeknown to me, had a daughter living in the UK. To cut a long story short, that one connection is what led me to my first job in the financial district in London.

Starting with why empowers your networking strategy

Starting with why lays the foundation of your networking strategy as it helps others understand and connect with you on a more profound level. Simon Sinek's book *Start With Why* focuses on how companies who concentrate on this deeper question are more competitive in the marketplace. Like many concepts I discuss in this book, I've taken this business approach and applied it to individuals. *Why* do you do what you do? What is your higher purpose?

By connecting with the core of who you are, others will like you and trust you. Your uniqueness then comes through in your conversations, dialogue, interviews, etc. You can explain, 'This is where my interest comes from. This is where I want to make a difference.' Your big 'why' is your personal touch, your story, your humanity that makes your connection with others truly unique and personal. It's much easier to engage in a conversation that's bigger than you. It's not about self-interest. You're articulating the impact you want to have and why that's meaningful. Others will be inspired by your clarity and honesty.

To help you think about your own 'why', here are a few questions to consider: What personal traits do you use to overcome challenges? Which activities reflect you at your best? What are your most memorable career moments and why? In what ways are you making an impact? What projects showcase your skills, talents and values? Your answers to these questions will help you understand yourself better and help you to articulate your 'why', allowing you to more easily connect with others.

Networking is the bridge to tomorrow

Given the power of networking, wouldn't it be a good idea to ensure you let others know what interests you, and perhaps what you'd like to get involved in, when you introduce yourself? Introductions are a perfect occasion to plant that initial seed in other people's minds about your potential. Let's take my client Clara as an example. Clara was preparing for a career transition after having worked for the same energy company for the last two decades. We were working together on her career transition plan, and her networking strategy was of course an integral part of that plan.

'I'm curious Clara, how do you introduce your-self?' I asked.

'It's quite straightforward,' she replied. 'I say, "I'm a geologist and I work for an energy com-pany."'

'Hmm,' I pondered out loud. 'How might you tweak your introduction to give others a hint about what you'd like to do in the future? What are you really excited about in your profession?'

Clara paused. After playing around with a few phrases she exclaimed, 'I work as a geologist for an energy company and I'm looking to get more involved in applying new technologies to geological challenges.'

I'm not a geologist and I'm not a technologist, but that sounds intriguing. Additionally, the way Clara phrased her introduction makes the listener curious and eager to ask further questions. What type of challenges? What type of technologies? It's easy for the dialogue to continue to develop. Clara also kept her intro-duction short and simple, which makes it easy for the listener to absorb and process. Less is more when it comes to introductions.

Notice how Clara subtly included her 'why'. Clara's 'why' was applying her years of training in geology – a field she loved – to solve the industry's problems, One of which is the high cost of energy exploration. Geologists are required to travel to explore sites. Additionally, not all areas are necessarily accessible to humans, thus leading to guesswork about the full exploration potential (for oil and minerals) of a given site. Clara's interest in geological challenges goes to the heart of who she is. She's a keen learner. She is willing to take a risk and learn about emerging technologies to investigate whether technological applications could make exploration cheaper and more productive. Clara is analytical and likes to solve problems – this is where she gets her energy from and what attracted her to the field of geology in the first place. It's amazing how her short introduction gives a flavour of all these qualities.

As Clara expanded her network internally, she practised her revised introduction. The more she shared her interest in new technologies, the more access she gained to other areas of the company that were involved in testing them. Although she was able to get involved in these new developments, however, the pace of change wasn't quick enough for her ambition.

Consequently, she ended up leaving her long-time employer and set up her own company. Clara's company uses drone and virtual reality technology to allow geologists to do their work a hundred times more cheaply and productively. It is now possible to access an entire potential exploration site without ever having to be there. Clara now introduces herself in this way: 'I'm a geologist by trade and have set up my own company to leverage drone and virtual reality technology to transform energy exploration.' Just like Clara, as your career grows and develops, the way you introduce yourself will evolve as well.

What's your story?

Our attention spans are decreasing at an alarming rate. We're overloaded with information, bombarded with work requests and overwhelmed with keeping our work and life plates spinning. Consequently, it's important to quickly and succinctly let others know about you. What's your story? Draft a short script or interesting sound bite. It's not necessary to be 100% certain about your career strategy, but you do need to have an idea of the *direction*. When I was transitioning from a corporate career to setting up my own career consultancy business, I was at pains to introduce myself. It was so easy to introduce myself when I was in the corporate world – things seemed more certain, clear and well defined. When I was transitioning, there was much that was up in the air, which made it hard for me to feel confident introducing myself. I was in the throes of launching my own business, but hadn't yet done it, and I didn't know exactly what the business would look like, so I felt insecure talking about it. Through trial and error, I was able to create a workable story: 'This is an exciting time for me. I'm thinking of writing a book about combining work and life, and then setting up a career consultancy business to help women enjoy both their personal and professional lives.' Notice I included the why – 'to help women enjoy their personal and professional lives'.

I was amazed by the amount of information and insight I gained by networking and using this approach. I met several authors who provided advice on how to write and how to publish. I received first-hand feedback that the concept of the book was a winner. Conversations led to further relevant contacts who could help me learn more about coaching and professional development. When I eventually started writing the book, I was still unclear about what the consultancy would look like, so my introduction evolved: 'This is an exciting time for me. I'm in the process of writing a book about combining work and life, and then will focus on setting up a career consultancy business to help women enjoy both their personal and professional lives.' That introduction led to speaking engagements before the book was even published. That's the power of an introduction – let others know where you're headed, and they'll be eager to help.

One of the hardest parts of crafting an introduction is identifying phrases that feel and sound natural rather than scripted like a CV. Here are some examples to kick off your own thought processes:

- I'm at a really interesting juncture in my life where I'm looking to get more involved in... (topic) – it seems fascinating.

- I'm exploring/considering... (role) – after many years doing... (job), I'm keen to look at opportunities in... (company or industry).

- My company is in growth mode with a focus on… (customers/market/products), and I'm looking to focus more on…

- One of the most exciting changes in my industry is… (development), and I'm looking to transition my career to be more aligned to this growth area.

Remember to be relaxed and casual when you're doing your introduction – nothing too serious, just a relaxed conversation. That's not to say this is easy. You may want to practise at home to get comfortable if you're incorporating new language about where you'd like to move to going forward. You need others to hear that you're confident and thoughtful about the direction in which you're headed.

Turning networking into career opportunities

My niece Tamara sought my advice about how to land a role she had her heart set on. She had just finished a year working for Teach America and now wanted to move into fundraising. She mentioned that she had been successful connecting with individuals working in fundraising but was having trouble taking it to the next level. She was not having any success getting others to respond to her messages to schedule one-on-one meetups after their initial introduction.

'What am I doing wrong, Aunt Chris?' The director of a political fundraising group (which Tamara was keen to work for) was not responding to her emails. Tamara was puzzled by this lack of response as she felt she had developed an excellent rapport during their first encounter.

I probed. 'Tamara, what is one of the biggest challenges this lady has in her role?'

'Ah, that's easy Aunt Chris. She's desperate to launch a digital marketing campaign. Her organisation lacks that skillset.'

'Perfect', I replied, 'Is that something you might be able to help her with? Could you give her some ideas on what to do and could you maybe offer some free help?'

'Yes, to all of the above,' replied Tamara with a renewed sense of enthusiasm in her voice. After our chat, Tamara emailed the director with the subject line, 'How to launch your digital marketing strategy'. The director rang her within twenty minutes of sending the email. Following up with people who you want to work for is most effective when you put yourself in their shoes. Don't expect them to have figured out how you can help them. Make it obvious. Draft your communication in a way that directly speaks to what they need. You'll be sure to get a quick response, just like my niece.

Candida works in the digital start-up area of a large technology consulting firm. When I first began working with her, she told me she had a silly dream. She wanted to move out of her traditional consulting role rolling out large software programmes, which she had been doing for the last twenty years. She was ready to 'put her skates on' now that her daughter was grown. Her interest in technology had not waned throughout her career, but the landscape was changing. She was bored of the humdrum project managing software rollouts and was keen to transition into the start-up area.

'You always want to leverage what you already have. Given your long tenure at the company and the reputation you have built, are there any areas of the company focusing on start-ups?' I queried.

'Yes, there is, but I don't know anyone in that group, there are no open roles and there's no hiring budget,' responded Candida despondently.

'Do you know who heads up the group?' I continued.

'Yes, I know of her but have never met her,' replied Candida.

I pushed on, 'What does the head of the group need?'

'Well,' pondered Candida, 'I know through a friend that knows her that she's struggling to get a handle on all the various potential start-ups who could be partnering with our traditional clients. She really could use someone to come in and set up a database and report back to the group on the live opportunities.'

'Is that something you could do as a side-of-the-desk work?' I nudged.

'Of course,' responded Candida confidently.

'Well, there's your answer,' I advised, 'Contact the head and let her know you'd like to talk to her about an idea you have for supporting the expansion of her group.'

The head of the group gladly accepted Candida's invitation to meet up. Six months after that initial meet-up, a role was created for Candida and she transitioned to that role full time. Candida was amazed.

'Christine, I had no contacts, there was no role and there was no budget and here I am working in my dream job.'

'That's the magic of identifying a need and knowing how to address it. Congratulations on your new role, Candida!'

MY ACTION PLAN

1. My story is… (Hint: what direction you want to move into and your 'why')
2. Given my story, the top three to five people I am going to connect with are…
3. The open-ended (exploratory) questions I'm going to ask during the conversation are…

References

Cialdini, Robert B, *Influence: The Psychology of Persuasion*, revised edition, Harper Business, 2007.

Eblin, Scott, '6 Ways to Become a Better Listener', *FastCompany.com*, 2017, https://fastcompany .com/3068959/6-ways-to-become-a-better -listener [accessed 22 November 2019].

Fine, Debra, *The Fine Art of Small Talk: How to Start a Conversation in Any Situation*, Piatkus, 2006.

Grant, Adam, *Give and Take*, Weidenfeld & Nicolson, 2013.

Marr, Bernard, '10 Important Career Lessons Most People Learn Too Late in Life', *Observer. com* 2016, https://observer.com/2016/09/ten -important-career-lessons-most-people-learn -too-late-in-life [accessed 22 November 2019].

Sinek, Simon, *Start With Why: How Great Leaders Inspire Everyone to Take Action*, Penguin, 2011.

Taylor, Claire, *The 12 Secrets to Influencing With Story*, The Story Mill, 2015.

Revere Relationships

Are you making the time to connect with others and build sustainable relationships within your workplace? Is it a struggle sometimes to figure out how to approach more senior colleagues? And have you seen others succeed in progressing their career while on the face of it, they seem less qualified? The more senior we become, the less important our hard work becomes. In the last chapter we discussed initial strategies to connect with someone – to network. This chapter delves deeper into how to build and enhance those relationships once that connection is made. In a business environment where working across disciplines, geographies and cultures has become commonplace,

problems may only be solved through collaboration and teamwork. The world is too complicated to work in silos. In the Industrial Age,
the unit of work was the individual. Now, in
the Information Age, the unit of work is the
team. Relationships and leadership go hand
in hand. Effective leadership – getting others
to follow your vision – demands the ability to
build rapport.

We choose people we know and trust

Let's assume you're a leader or manager operating in chaos. You're under pressure and anxious
about your own future in the organisation. How
would you select a new operational team tasked
with moving the organisation forward with
the new strategy? Would your preference be
to choose someone you knew and trusted or
someone you didn't know, but who appeared
to have superior qualifications? Let's be honest – we all choose people we know and trust
first and foremost. In uncertain times, trust is
paramount. There are so many unpredictable
variables. You want to select people whom you
can trust, creating certainty in an uncertain
world. This is the most important selection

criteria. Trust trumps experience and qualifications every time.

During one of the many reorganisations that I survived, I recall the new head of department bringing in his own business manager. The problem for me was that I was already the business manager of the department. In a meeting of eight managers, it was announced that Marilyn was now the business manager of the group and I was reporting to her. My face turned red. No one had bothered to tell me. Upon reflection, it's clear the decision had nothing to do with my competence or track record. It had everything to do with the fifteen-year history Marilyn had working with the new head of department at their prior firm. It's nearly impossible not to take these situations personally, but they're not intended as a judgement on you.

To navigate through this sticky situation, I thought about how I could leverage my knowledge of the company and my longstanding relationships for Marilyn's benefit. I came to respect Marilyn's wider experience in project management and risk analysis, especially in derivates. We learned from each other. Due to family illness, Marilyn's tenure was brief – less than two years. In the end, she recommended me as her replacement. I then earned back the role which had been taken away. With the right mindset, there's always something to learn in a tough situation. The biggest lesson for me was that trust drives most decisions, particularly when it relates to people, such as performance reviews, new hires, redundancies, selection of service providers, etc. In business we sometimes fool ourselves that hard facts drive our decision-making. The truth is, we simply use the data to back up a decision we've already made based on our gut, which is principally based on trust.

Evaluate relationships through your strategic lens

Use a strategic lens to determine which relationships matter the most given where you want to go and what you're trying to achieve. Those are the relationships you really need to nurture to a level of trust and respect. A targeted approach saves you time. It's not possible to develop deep, strong relationships with everyone, nor is it necessary for your success. While you're executing the day job and developing relationships with current stakeholders, remember to connect with others outside of your area to plant the seeds for future opportunities.

Connie, a busy lawyer with a young family, was up for partner in her law firm. We chatted through her plan to secure the promotion and how it needed to be targeted in order to be effective. She was crystal clear on her business case. Her technical expertise and ability to deliver were solid. She knew that she also had to demonstrate her ability to grow the practice. She had a target list of clients with whom she was starting to develop more business and was confident there were plenty more opportunities to harness.

'How about the key decision makers and influencers in the firm?' I asked.

With this question, Connie took a moment to reflect and then disclosed, 'My reporting partner is very supportive.'

'Connie, you don't want to leave any stone unturned. Support from your manager is a given. It's essential to think strategically about the relationships you need to bring on board to get the promotion over the line,' I encouraged. As we chatted, Connie realised that she needed to speak to each partner and share her business plan. The firm was small enough that that was feasible. Each partner would be voting on her promotion; thus, each partner deserved a conversation. The partners were impressed with her plan and the way she actively lobbied for her promotion. Connie is now a partner.

The difference between coaches, mentors and sponsors

There's much confusion concerning the differences between coaches, mentors and sponsors. It's important to sort this out so you are clear on what you may need and who might be best placed to fulfil that need. While mentors and sponsors may use coaching techniques, such as asking insightful questions to provoke self-reflection, they are not coaches. A coach helps you identify and set goals in a particular area and develop a plan to achieve those goals. Through questioning and self-reflection, the coachee takes full ownership of his or her goals, plans and actions. A coach, for instance, may help you with putting together a strategy on how to increase your visibility and gain the support of mentors and sponsors. Coaching is a paid profession, is independent from the organisation you work for and is confidential.

The biggest difference between mentors and sponsors is that mentors offer you *insight* while sponsors give you *opportunities*. Sponsors are influencers and power brokers within your organisation or industry and their support of your career is visible. Mentors and sponsors serve different purposes, but they can be complementary. For example, mentors can prepare you for sponsorship. Be careful though – if you only have mentors in your network, you're unlikely to get the career acceleration you're looking for as it's the sponsors who will open doors to the next level. The more you think about *how* you want a mentor or sponsor to help you, the more targeted you can be on whom to connect with. Where do you want to go? You don't need to know exactly but you should have an idea of the general path. It's important to keep in mind that no single mentor or sponsor will meet all your criteria or your needs. It's ok if they don't look or act like you. Mentors and sponsors are not supermen and women. Each will have their strengths and weaknesses.

How to use mentors

Mentors are adept at expanding and clarifying career options. They can help you improve your subject matter expertise and industry knowledge. They listen, serve as a sounding board and encourage reflection. They have insight into what's *really* needed to get to the next level and understand how to navigate the political landscape. Mentors prepare you to be ready to gain a sponsor or sponsors by helping you articulate your goals clearly and succinctly. The more you talk about where you want to go, the more you're able to refine your thinking by taking on board the mentor's observations and feedback. Mentors can be current or former colleagues, former bosses, members of industry associations, school or university alumni, charity connections, former clients, former suppliers or members of your local sports clubs. A mentor should not be in your direct reporting line. They should be independent from those who have direct influence on your performance evaluation.

Once I set my sights on promotion to Managing Director, I realised that I needed a mentor to help me navigate the intricacies of climbing up that next slippery rung of the career ladder. My boss was extremely supportive of my promotion, but I knew I needed more independent advice and greater visibility outside my department. Managing directors are expected to have relationships across functions and upwards. I thought perhaps someone who sat on the bank's executive committee could be a smart choice. Was there someone who logically I could engage with on business topics and then steer on to career advice and guidance?

The light bulb went off – the head of credit, Denis, fit the bill. I respected his opinion, he was mild-mannered, and a calm and considered character, especially under pressure. He was outside my department, so my reporting line did not cross into his area. I considered him a colleague and knew him through various business interactions but hadn't spent the time developing the relationship. I was clear on what I needed – I wasn't looking for him to open doors the way a sponsor would. I was, however, looking for someone who was seasoned and had a reputation for excellence and professionalism.

Denis was a reliable and solid sounding-board for business issues, such as how best to develop new markets. He helped me think through a multitude of angles and concerns beyond my department's aim of simply generating new revenue sources. He helped me develop the mindset of a senior executive rather than an individual performer. Denis enjoyed sharing his expertise and our chats were like university tutor sessions – complete eye-openers. I felt more comfortable sticking to business issues at first as opposed to talking about myself and my career goals. Those discussions, however, did offer a variety of opportunities to touch upon softer development topics, such as how to influence others.

To my surprise, Denis then connected me to other mentors in the organisation. In this way, he helped increase my visibility and reputation for hard work and delivery. Without the support of Denis and the other mentors (whom he effectively recruited for me) I would not have been able to develop into a senior executive. Working harder would not have changed things. The main reason I would not categorise Denis and the other mentors as sponsors was their lack of influence to push for my promotion. While their opinions were respected, they were not the types who would bang the table and stick their necks out when it came to promotions. They operated more like my secret weapon, guiding me in the right way from behind the scenes. I would simply not have had the cross-functional relationships, nor the broader strategic view of the business that was necessary for a Managing Director candidate without the support of these mentors. They were crucial to my professional development.

How to use sponsors

Sponsors can intervene directly to move your career forward – helping you get selected for high-profile projects as well as earn a pay rise or promotion. Sponsors give you first-hand feedback on your leadership, management and executive presence. They watch your back and protect you from political dangers. They use their visibility to increase yours. They promote you to influencers and power brokers, whom they have credibility with as they are influencers and power brokers themselves. In real life, the differences between mentors and sponsors can get blurred – that's ok. In corporate life, there's more grey than black and white. A mentor, for instance, can become a sponsor and vice versa. You could have a sponsor who not only opens doors for you but who is also giving you advice like a mentor would. To be successful, we all need someone else to open doors and share their insights and visibility of opportunities in the wider organisation. Sponsors are skilled in offensive and defensive play. They see danger way before we have an inkling of the hazards.

The sponsor who had the biggest impact on my corporate career was Mazz. Mazz was a mentor, then boss, sponsor, and friend. I first met Mazz in the late eighties when he spoke at a US Treasury conference in London that I had organised. Mazz was a seasoned banker from New York and had recently been transferred to London. I, on the other hand, was a novice to the financial industry, having just landed a job as a conference manager in London. At the end of that conference, Mazz came up to me and said, 'You don't want to be running plain vanilla US Treasury conferences. The repo [secured short-term money market product] is a well-developed product in the US but is just emerging in Europe. You want to be running repo conferences.' Mazz shared his first-hand knowledge and insight into the financial industry and recommended additional resources to help me progress up the learning curve. He was a mentor showing me the ropes. We went on to collaborate on four highly successful repo conferences during my two-year tenure in London.

In 1990, I moved back to the US to complete an MBA in International Business. Upon graduation, I contacted Mazz about potential job opportunities in London. (By then I really did understand international finance.) Mazz had just switched banks and was looking to expand his repo trading desk from inter-bank to institutional clients.

'With your sales and project management skills, educational background, combined with foreign language capabilities, you'd be a perfect candidate to lead our sales and marketing effort.' Mazz then became my boss. When I first joined the bank, Mazz spent a lot of time explaining the ins and outs of fixed income markets. Even though he was a boss, he demonstrated strong mentorship qualities through his management style. He was always on the lookout to connect me with senior people, increase my visibility and develop me. Unfortunately, my experience is that many managers lack the talent or interest to develop others – they are so focused on delivering their objectives, there's little time to think about developing others.

Mazz left the bank two years after I had joined. Five years later, he became a sponsor. He effectively recruited me for a business manager role for one of his closest friends at another bank. I was not looking for a job. I was hand-picked. I had no experience in business management. Mazz promoted me to his friend, claiming that I had the skill set to be his 'right hand man'. As sponsors do, Mazz put his own reputation on the line when he put my name forward as a potential candidate for the role. Mazz recognised that it would stretch me and set me up for leadership roles, something I wouldn't appreciate until many years later. Even though sponsors are usually within your organisation, they can also be former bosses outside your company. The bottom line is that there are no hard and fast lines between mentors and sponsors. My recommendation is to use all resources at hand but be sure you have sponsors as they can open doors.

Making the initial approach

Reaching out to potential mentors and sponsors can be daunting. What do I actually say when making that initial approach? To initiate your own thinking process, here are a few phrases to consider which are intended to be delivered in a casual manner:

- I was really interested to hear your views about… (recent meeting, presentation, etc) – I'd love to get thirty minutes in your diary to explore.

- Your career journey is fascinating, I'd appreciate thirty minutes to learn more about…

- Given your area of expertise, I'd welcome your input on…

- I understand you're heading up … (project, eg) – I'd really like to understand the needs/challenges of the project and see how I might help.

- I see that you've been appointed as the new head of our corporate charity project. I'd like to understand your priorities and wonder if you could share some of your experiences to date.

The more specifics you can include that relate to the person you're approaching, the more success you're likely to have. They will be interested in you as you're showing genuine interest in them – tailor your phrases as much as possible to the individual. I'm not a fan of meeting someone for the first time and them saying, 'Will you be my mentor, or will you be my sponsor?' For me, this feels premature and forced. You haven't built up the relationship. In my own mentor and sponsor relationships, I never asked that question. The relationship developed in a natural way. In contrast, when someone asked me to be their mentor on first meeting, it felt awkward and uncomfortable. We hardly knew each other, so it scared me. How could I take on this responsibility? That being said, companies have distinct cultures, and company-sponsored mentor and sponsorship programmes follow separate guidelines. Go with what works in your organisation and what's on offer.

It's a two-way street

Mentorships and sponsorships are the ultimate career-enhancing relationships, and like any relationship, both parties should benefit. As the mentee or person looking for sponsorship, the burden is on you to give first. Think about them. What could you do for them? Perhaps you are wondering what you could possibly have to offer these senior individuals? As mentioned under Rule 4 ('Nourish Your Network'), asking them for input or advice or showing interest in their career path is a form a giving – you're paying a compliment to the other person. You're saying, 'I value your opinion and experience.' Be creative. Perhaps you could help set up or improve the senior person's LinkedIn profile or social media presence. Perhaps you have information about what's happening at the lower echelons of the organisation which could be useful for them to know. Perhaps you have some recommendations on sporting activities or holidays for which you know the other person shares the same interest.

Even though it's a two-way street, you are the one who is expected to keep the dialogue going, to follow up and schedule appointments. Mentors tend to mentor because they enjoy giving back. They get a lot of fulfilment seeing others develop. Sponsors sponsor because you make them look good. Sponsorship is visible. Sponsors also benefit from an expanded reach within the organisation, which helps them get things done. Sponsorship might also be tied to performance evaluations, where there's an expectation to develop talent and future leaders. You're the sponsor's protégé. You don't need to feel like a beggar. Sponsors and mentors benefit from the relationship as well and they would have had mentors and sponsors who facilitated their own career progression.

Once Candida finally got the promotion to senior manager that she had wanted for ten years, she exclaimed, 'If only I had known earlier in my career how vital sponsorship is to promotion! For so many years I've been working hard and doing well, but never quite clinching the next level up.' After transitioning to the digital start-up area, Candida advanced as she continued to discover more of the unwritten rules. The secret to her promotion was her ability to align her success to that of the influential executives in her field. Sponsors lend their support and reputation to less experienced professionals whom they believe add value and can help them be successful. Promotions are therefore a two-way street as well.

Your aim is to earn the trust of your mentor and sponsor and keep up your end of bargain, which is continuing to work hard and deliver quality output. It also means you should be watching the mentor's or sponsor's back. What are you hearing or seeing that could be harmful to them or their department? Because a sponsor is putting their neck on the line, your sponsor will certainly be putting you through some tests as well. Through the performance of your role, and the manner in which you perform it – your professionalism and integrity – you will gain the trust of the mentor or sponsor. Sponsorship is out in the open. Sponsors are risking their reputation for you. When trust is broken, don't expect the sponsor to be supportive and understanding. They will drop you like a hot potato! You are an extension of them. If you lose their trust, they will want to minimise their risks and disassociate themselves from you as quickly as possible. Building a relationship with a mentor and sponsor is a process, rather than a one-shot deal. Be patient, persistent and positive in nurturing that relationship.

MY ACTION PLAN

1. My career goal is to...
2. In light of my career goal, the names of my principal stakeholders are...
3. The relationships with stakeholders which I need to enhance further are...
4. In order to build/enhance the relationships noted above, I am going to take the following actions...

Tip: Make a note in your diary each week to take specific actions to enhance your key relationships – ie schedule pop-in chats, coffee or lunch, etc.

References

Anderson, Rania, H, *WE: Men, Women, and the Decisive Formula for Winning at Work*, John Wiley & Sons, 2018.

Coleman, Harvey J, *Empowering Yourself: The Organizational Game Revealed*, 2nd edition, AuthorHouse, 2010.

Dalai Lama, and Tutu, Desmond, with Abrams, Douglas, *The Book of Joy*, Hutchinson, 2016.

Foust-Cummings, Heather, and Dinolfo, Sarah, 'Report: Sponsoring Women to Success', *Catalyst*, 2011, https://catalyst.org/research/sponsoring -women-to-success [accessed 22 November 2019].

Grant, Adam, *Give and Take*, Weidenfeld & Nicolson, 2013.

Ibarra, Herminia, and Kirkby, Julia 'Women are Over-Mentored (But Under-Sponsored)', *Harvard Business Review*, 2010, https://hbr.org/2010/08/women-are-over-mentored-but-un [accessed 22 November 2019].

Hewlett, Sylvia Ann, 'Mentors are Good. Sponsors are Better.', *New York Times*, 2013, https://nytimes.com/2013/04/14/jobs/sponsors-seen-as-crucial-for-womens-career-advancement.html [accessed 22 November 2019].

Sotomayor, Sonia, *My Beloved World*, reprint edition, Vintage Books, 2014.

Wittenberg-Cox, Avivah, *How Women Mean Business: A Step by Step Guide to Profiting from Gender Balanced Business*, John Wiley & Sons, 2010.

RULE #6

Navigate Negotiations

Do you find it easier to negotiate on behalf of others than to negotiate for your own benefit? If you do, you're not alone. Many of us perform better when we're advocating for others rather than ourselves, particularly when it comes to pay or promotion. Asking for what we want can feel awkward and uncomfortable. The secret is learning to negotiate and to ask for what you want in a way where everyone feels like they've won. I am a realist. This isn't some fanciful idea. It really does work. I am a converted negotiator. Like most things, it didn't happen overnight – it was a process. The more you practise, the more it forms part of your everyday behaviour. I used to shy away from speaking up. I thought I was meant to listen in performance discussions and to be grateful for any pay rise or promotion that came my way. I believed that my manager knew best. If my manager mentioned that the firm had had a tough year, I would almost feel guilty if I got a raise. This is flawed reasoning. Negotiating for a win–win deal is not only possible, but also with practice, it can feel so natural that you aren't even conscious that you're doing it.

One day I was working in the office and a fax was coming through on the machine several seats away from my seat. I thought I'd be help-ful, so I got up retrieved the fax and started reading it to determine whom it was intended for. As I sifted through the details, I realised the fax was a copy of an approved application for renting a flat. The application itself included detailed salary and bonus information for my colleague Carlos. Although I was more senior than Carlos in terms of title and responsibility, he was making tens of thousands of pounds more than I was. Carlos wasn't in the office when the fax came through, so I stuck it in an envelope and placed it under his keyboard and never said a word.

In those days gender diversity, the gender pay gap, or equal pay for equal work were not common terminology (note: this organisation no longer exists). My instinct was not to go to Human Resources. Instead, I waited until my performance review three months later. During those three months I diligently prepared the business case for the raise I was going to ask for. To calculate a fair amount, I took my colleague's base and bonus and increased my own by 20%. My business case revolved around the sales results I had delivered and how well-positioned I was to continue that trajectory, which was in line with the firm's strategy.

After three long months, it was time to meet up with my manager for the annual performance review. I gave a detailed and thorough summary of my revenue contribution and articulated my goals and objectives for the coming year. I then added, 'Given this stellar performance, I think a 20% increase in my total compensation would be reasonable.' Dead silence. It felt like hours before I heard a reply. Finally, after an excruciating wait, my manager chirped, 'Fine, no problem.' And that was the end of that. No questions, no pushback, nothing – just 'fine'. You may be thinking, 'That's easy for you Christine. You're confident and not afraid to speak up.' That's the case now, but that certainly was not the case then. I have grown to be more confident and comfortable speaking up. In fact, I have grown to truly enjoy the challenge of negotiating, especially figuring out how the negotiation can benefit others.

Asking changes everything

Today, most managers are consumed by their own survival. They simply have little time to think about the development of others or what others want or need. That's why asking changes everything. It's essential for gaining the resources and opportunities necessary for career advancement. No one is served by keeping you small. You're a professional. You own your career. You want to the best you can be. No more excuses then – the onus is on you to think about what you need to be successful. Your manager is busy. He or she is also not a mind-reader. A true professional is expected to think strategically. What is the impact you want to have that is aligned to the department or company's goals? It's up to you to assess the gap between where you are now and your desired destination.

Melinda credits learning how to ask for what she wanted as the single biggest factor in progressing to the C-suite. She learned the hard way that success requires more than working harder and longer and exceeding performance metrics. Even if you meet or exceed the agreed targets, you will still need to ask for any kind of reward in return. Performance alone – including exceptional performance – keeps you stuck. Melinda decided to transition to a securities regulator after years working at one of the large international law firms. This was a big change. Melinda had only ever worked in a law firm. She thought she'd better find out the rules of the game and how you get promoted within the regulator sooner rather than later.

Melinda checked with her boss shortly after her arrival. 'How can I be successful here? What does success at the regulator require?' Her boss replied, 'Ah, that's really straightforward Melinda. It's not like a law firm. We are very transparent. Your performance rating will be based on the number of legal cases you close. The more cases you close, the higher your rating. It's that simple.' Famous last words. Melinda worked tirelessly to make that happen. At the end of the performance cycle, Melinda had closed more cases than anyone in her department – 40% more, to be exact.

Year-end promotions were announced. Melinda's name was nowhere to be seen on the published promotion list. How could this be? She was doubly surprised when she saw her colleague's name, John, on the list. She was stumped and devastated. John had closed significantly fewer cases. Melinda gathered the courage to have lunch with John, with whom she had a good working relationship. Over lunch she pried, 'John, how did you get promoted? I thought the promotions were based on the number of cases closed.' John responded in a calm and collected manner, 'That was easy, Melinda. I just kept telling our direct boss as well as all the managers in the other departments that I wanted to get promoted. And while my numbers maybe weren't the highest, my ambition to move the next level was never in doubt.'

At that moment, Melinda grasped that she had to actually *ask* for a promotion regardless of how stellar her performance was. Because she hadn't asked, others assumed that she didn't want to be promoted. Perhaps they had made assumptions (with no harm intended) that she didn't want to get promoted at this juncture as she had a young family. Melinda now preaches, 'Everything is up for grabs, but you have to ask for it. And once you ask for it, the conversation continues.' Melinda recommends spending 80% of your role on the delivery and 20% on positioning your career for the next move or opportunity: 'Tell people what you want.' Having been burned once, Melinda always asks for what she wants. What's the worst that can happen? The downside of not asking makes the potential upside of asking quite attractive.

Melinda was in fact promoted the following year, when everyone knew about her ambition, and continued to work at the regulator for another couple of years. She was then ready to move into the private sector and through her targeted networking strategy, transitioned to Chief Risk Officer at an insurance company. The role was ideal – she was now in industry and was operating within the C-suite. One day, Melinda was updating the CEO on risk management issues when he paused and asked, 'Melinda, do you have a few more minutes? I'd like to share with you my thoughts around reorganising the business.' Melinda replied, 'Of course. I'd welcome the opportunity to gain more insight into the overall structure of the business.'.

The CEO placed a diagram on the table outlining the new organisational chart with various boxes indicating the name of the department along with the designated head. Melinda noticed that the box for head of financial institutions had not been filled in yet. Melinda pointed to it. 'This is the role I could do well.' The CEO reacted immediately. 'Hmm, I never thought of you for that role Melinda, but now that you mention it, I think you're right. Give me a bit more time to mull that one over.' Shortly thereafter, Melinda was promoted to the Head of Financial Institutions group, transitioning out of Risk Management into a client-facing business area.

The consequence of not asking is quite severe. It's a slippery slope, which eventually can completely derail you. If you don't negotiate, you eventually end up demotivated, which then impacts your performance. By not negotiating, it's more likely you won't get the recognition or opportunities you deserve. Demotivation culminates into lack of creativity, positive thinking and ability to solve problems. A negative mindset hurts collaboration and ability to navigate tricky interpersonal dynamics. Occasionally some of my coaching clients may push back and claim they are okay with not negotiating: 'Christine, the promotion and pay aren't the most important aspect of my work. It's the working relationships that matter to me. I know there are many others in the organisation that respect me, although my superiors don't fully appreciate my current value-add or potential.'

My experience is that eventually this lack of recognition bites back. Over time, the resentment builds up (worsened by seeing others less qualified than you get promoted), and you become angry and unhappy because you know you are capable of so much more. Frustration and anger further inhibit your ability to make a positive impact on those around you. Getting the appropriate recognition in terms of pay, title, promotion, professional development opportunities or other resources is unlikely. You have no choice but to ask and negotiate. Not asking makes you look more junior and less ambitious. Asking for what you want improves your chance of being in a role you find personally meaningful and where you're best placed to be at your optimum for your colleagues, clients and the company at large.

Know what's important to you

When negotiating, be clear on what you most want to attain (pleasure) or most want to avoid (pain). Pleasure in a work context could be flexibility in your work schedule which enables you to work from home, additional team support or financial rewards. Pain could be working weekends or extensive travel. Not only do we each have our unique needs and wants, those criteria evolve over time. Prioritise them. Which things are 'nice to have' as opposed to fundamental? Don't fall into the trap of assuming what you value, others do to the same degree, if at all. I remember when I started my new sales role in London, my boss requested that I travel to France two days a week for the next six months. 'You can't be serious,' I thought to myself, 'I've just moved my family here from the US. I'm just getting the kids settled in their new school and my husband is settling in his new job.' My boss added, 'Tell me what you need to make this happen.'

At that point in my career, I viewed travel as pain. That evening, I mentioned to my husband how ridiculous this request was. Encouragingly, he replied, 'Seems like a great opportunity for you. Think about how this could work.' Darn, I wasn't going to get out of this one easily. The question whirled around in my head, 'What did I need to make this happen?' The aspect I disliked the most about travelling was having to travel on a Sunday evening. It disrupted valuable family weekend time. Although technically I wouldn't have to travel until Sunday evening, I couldn't fully relax and enjoy the day. My proposal to the boss was to depart early Monday morning and return Tuesday evening. In that way, I'd only be away one night. The boss responded, 'Sounds good.' More money or a more senior title was not what I needed in that situation. When you're clear about what's important to you and you understand what's important to the other party, magic happens.

Prepare for likely objections

Considering what the likely objections will be is a fundamental part of preparation for any negotiation. So often we focus on our arguments without taking into account the perspective of the other person. How might they feel or react? What are the likely issues they will raise? If you're not ready for objections, it can really dampen your rhythm and momentum in negotiation. Your balloon will be popped and you'll have difficulty recovering. Expect that there will be objections. Given the other person's situation and circumstance, which objections are the most likely to be raised? From my days working in a Japanese culture, I learned that before any negotiation, it's beneficial to conduct due diligence behind the scenes. Who do you know who might have a better understanding of the perspective of the person you're about to negotiate with?

Once you've done your homework and understand the likely objections, it's time to think about your response to those objections. Again, seek feedback from trusted colleagues about your proposed responses. Don't worry if an issue comes up which takes you completely off guard. You can buy time by using your 'Get Out of Jail Free card'. In the board game Monopoly®, a 'Get Out of Jail Free' card releases you from jail and allows you to continue moving around the board buying and selling property. In a professional setting, a 'Get Out of Jail Free card' buys you time – it frees you from a tricky spot. Say something like: 'That's a valid point that deserves further consideration. I'll set up a follow-up meeting for further discussion once

I've been able to look into it.' Be sure to follow up. Your reputation is at stake.

Align interests to build rapport

We frequently go into a negotiation thinking we have all the answers, mostly because we're only thinking about ourselves. We think we know how the other party is going to react. We think we know what's important to them. To align interests and build rapport, try to unveil *why* the other party holds a certain view or position. Keep asking questions (in a gentle, positive manner) until the answer becomes clear. What is their most important objective? If you can ascertain that, perhaps you can concede on another point which meets that objective, which may not be an option the other party has considered. What is the other party's biggest concern or fear?

When our daughter was getting married several years ago, I was quite chuffed when she asked me to negotiate with the chosen venue. She said, 'Mum, this is your kind of thing. You're good at negotiating.' We wanted to keep within a certain budget and the package the venue proposed was over budget by several thousand pounds. I confidently shared with my daughter that I'm sure we could negotiate on the snack food scheduled to be served at 9.30pm. We had arranged an evening cocktail reception with hors d'œuvres followed by the wedding meal and dancing, which is when the snacks were due to be served. Surely there would be enough food for our guests already. Another serving of food at 9.30pm seemed over the top.

I fell into the trap. I thought I knew what was important to the venue. I reiterated our objective of cutting the cost by several thousand pounds and that we'd like to scrap the 9.30pm snack food. The venue was obstinate. They would not budge on the evening snack. How could I have got this so wrong? How did I not read the situation better? I forgot to determine the *why* behind their obstinance. The venue had hosted hundreds of weddings over the years and they found that guests would complain if there was no food served during the dancing part of the evening (after a lot of alcohol had been served). Those complaints hurt the venue's reputation. The venue, on the other hand, understood the reason behind our request to eliminate the late evening snack – ie to reduce the costs. Therefore, they suggested we serve prosecco instead of champagne and choose a less expensive menu for the main meal. These were excellent suggestions, neither of which had crossed our minds. It was the perfect compromise. It was a win–win. Our interests were aligned.

At no point during these discussions was either party rude or disrespectful. We had built up a good rapport even though we weren't in full agreement on the details. They listened to our concerns and objectives. I listened to theirs. Listening builds rapport. It's so frustrating when you're working through an issue with someone and all they do is repeat their position, over and over again, seemingly not taking any of your points into consideration. The other party is failing to address the objections you're raising, hoping instead that you'll forget and simply agree with the proposal they have repeated multiple times. It's infuriating and unproductive.

Be sure to benchmark your requests

If you ask for too little, you'll look junior and give the impression that you don't value your own abilities. If you ask for too much, you'll look ill-informed and unprepared. It's incumbent on you to benchmark your request. What are others asking for in a similar situation? If it's pay, investigate the market rate. There are some terrific online resources nowadays such as Glassdoor, Salary.com, Indeed and Payscale. Additionally, think about individuals you know who might be able give you some general guidance or ranges.

When I was negotiating my salary for my first banking job in London, that's exactly what I did. I contacted my old boss, Sue, who headed up the financial conference company I had previously worked for and asked her. She didn't have that information to hand, but certainly had contacts in finance who would know. Sue came back with a range across different roles and levels of seniority. It was just what I needed. It gave me at least a ballpark for where I should pitch my salary requirements. If you're looking for a raise within your current organisation, build advocacy internally around what you're asking for. Do others support your request? Is it reasonable and at the right level? Is your timing right? Are there other people within the organisation whom you may need to bring on board?

Know your bottom line

Know what your bottom line is and be prepared to walk away to defend it. Bluffing is a dangerous strategy. Being dishonest about what you want and when you're prepared to walk away undermines your credibility, particularly for any future negotiations. Recently my friend Yanna contacted her mobile phone provider and told them she was going to switch to another provider who offered a lower price. The bottom line was set – if the company didn't lower the cost, Yanna would terminate her contract. The customer service rep inquired, 'What rates are you seeing with alternative providers?' Dead silence.

Yanna had not researched any alternatives. She had heard from colleagues that if you ring the mobile phone company and say you're leaving, they will reduce the price of your contract. Yanna improvised. 'I've seen a number of offers which are at least £15 a month cheaper.' The rep carried on, 'Not sure we can match that. Could you provide more details on the specific offers you've seen?' Yanna's bottom line wasn't genuine, and she'd been found out. The company said it wasn't able to reduce her bill at this time.

Yanna is still with the same provider and is on record for making an insincere attempt at terminating her contract.

Leveraging outcomes

When you approach negotiating in the right way, following the principles in this chapter, you never lose, regardless of the outcome. Negotiating gives you the opportunity to learn. Maybe you didn't get exactly what you wanted (at least not this time), but you will have learned something about the situation, the other person, or yourself. Or maybe you were successful, but you've discovered things that will make the next round of negotiating even easier. Negotiating is not a one-shot deal. If the other person is clear that if certain conditions were met, the no could turn into a maybe, or even a yes, it's your responsibility to keep them apprised of your progress in meeting their conditions. You'll be preparing them for the day when you say, 'That's now happened, so let's talk about the next step.'

When you get a no to your request for a pay rise or a promotion, confirm what conditions need to be met in order for it to happen. Don't wait until the end of the year to communicate that the conditions are now met so you're expecting that raise or promotion. Keep your manager up to date on your progress in meeting those conditions throughout the year. Hold the manager accountable. Your expectations will be transparent and you will have solicited regular feedback on your performance, maximising your chances of getting the conclusion you want by year-end.

MY ACTION PLAN

1. The scenario I want to negotiate is…

2. The reason this is important to me is because…

3. Even though there are likely to be objections (which I have considered), the other party can benefit from my request in that…

4. I will do the following due diligence to prepare for my negotiations…

5. Although I will follow a solutions-oriented approach, I am clear that my bottom line is…

References

Camp, Jim, 'Decisions Are Largely Emotional, Not Logical: The Neuroscience Behind Decision-making', *Big Think*, 2012, https://bigthink.com/experts-corner/decisions-are-emotional-not-logical-the-neuroscience-behind-decision-making [accessed 22 November 2019].

Frumin, Lisa, 'What Do You Want? Just Ask For it', 2017, https://medium.com/@lisa_80738/what-do-you-want-just-ask-for-it-9a9e36c3613a [accessed 22 November 2019].

Kellaway, Lucy, 'How to Ask for What You Want – And Get It Every Time', *Financial Times*, 2017, https://ft.com/c°ntent/2053f906-e98d-11e6-893c-082c54a7f539 [accessed 22 November 2019].

Reynolds, Natalie, *We Have a Deal: How to Negotiate with Intelligence, Flexibility and Power*, Icon Books, 2016.

Thomason, Bobbi, 'Women's Career Negotiations', 2016, https://youtube.com/watch?v=jHAOdEbjs_8 [accessed 22 November 2019].

Tinsley, Catherine H, 'GUWLI Leadership Development Series: Negotiating for Success', 2015, https://youtube.com/watch?v=Q3rjN4S73 -0 [accessed 22 November 2019].

Wekelo, Kerry Alison, *Culture Infusion: 9 Principles to Create and Maintain a Thriving Organizational Culture*, Zendoway, 2017.

Cherish Challenging Conversations

Do you shy away from having conversations that are truly uncomfortable, whether they be about a pay rise, performance or a particular conflict? Have you ever practised the conversation in your head, and in the end hesitated to actually deliver the message as the timing no longer seemed ideal? While having difficult conversations may seem natural to others, it's really a skill any of us can learn, and the sooner the better. Not having the conversation doesn't resolve the issue. Arguably, it makes matters worse as we tend to internalise the stress, increasing our anxiety levels and decreasing our ability to be at our best. It's not the case that some of us are born with the talent to handle those challenging conversations head on, while others find it more difficult. This is not an innate skill. Everyone finds it difficult at first. It's a skill that with focus, experience and practice each of us can become expert at.

The other piece of good news is that regardless of the actual topic of the difficult conversation, the same methodology is applied to generate positive outcomes, so it is handy for your personal life as well as your professional life. When I first researched this topic for a workshop I was running, I typed into Google 'having' and up popped in spot number one, 'having difficult conversations'. That tells you something. You're not alone in struggling to have these awkward dialogues. People the world over are in a similar situation.

Difficult conversations lead to a pathway of growth

The irony is that it's the precisely the *difficult* conversations that we should be having. These are the ones that are game-changers in our lives, both personally and professionally. Kaitlynn was completely miffed that she didn't get the promotion to partner in the professional services firm she was working in. She received glowing feedback year in, year out. What was missing? Why did she not get the promotion? It was starting to feel like it would never happen. It felt like she was going to be a permanent director.

When I asked her what kind of feedback she had received the first time she was passed up for promotion to partner, she looked a bit puzzled. 'My performance reviews have all been very good.'

I commented, 'If you're not getting the promotion you want, you'll need to seek out tough feedback which will explain why you haven't nailed the promotion. Something isn't adding up.' I then proceeded to ask about the informal feedback process she pursued.

Again, another puzzled look, followed by, 'What do you mean informal feedback process?'

'Who are the people you ask during the year, not around performance reviews, about how you're doing, about what areas you need to improve?

Who are you asking specifically to sponsor your partnership application?'

Despondently, Kaitlynn answered, 'I don't see the point of informal feedback. Isn't that over-kill, as that's the purpose of the annual review and promotion process?' Kaitlynn was now intrigued. 'How does informal feedback work? Who should I go to?'

I suggested that she seek out colleagues who were courageous, who didn't necessarily fol-low the pack and whom she trusted. After a hard think, Kaitlynn decided to contact her colleague Sally for advice. Sally's advice was game-changing. Sally shared with Kaitlynn that she had perhaps unknowingly developed a reputation for not listening to and accepting feedback well. As a consequence, Kaitlynn's colleagues had given up sharing their honest feedback, including the more subtle and sen-sitives issues connected with partner promo-tions. Ironically, the ability to seek feedback and demonstrate self-correcting behaviour was in fact noted as one of the necessary qualities to becoming partner.

While Kaitlynn in her own mind was executing her task list beautifully and receiving positive feedback, others were simultaneously forming the view that she was not partner material but didn't dare share their views or reasoning for fear of 'getting their heads bitten off'. Thanks to Kaitlynn's generous colleague Sally, Kaitlynn is now fully aware of her obstacles to reach the next level and has put together a strategy to address the specific concerns raised. To her credit, she has also formed a wider inner circle of trusted colleagues in addition to Sally, who offer informal, genuine (yet sometimes harsh) feedback, as she realises this is the only way she'll know if she's moving in the right direction. Continuing to receive glowing annual reviews without getting to the hard truth was not going to help her achieve her goals.

Preparing for talks on pay and promotion

Without a doubt, when it comes to challenging conversations, knowing how to handle pay and promotion is at the top of the list. Through the webinars and workshops, I've run over the years, a common set of questions emerges: 'Where do I begin? How do I frame the conversation in a way that makes clear to my manager that I deserve a promotion? I've never had a pay-related conversation ever in my twenty-year career – tell me more. How do I prove my value as a part-time worker?' First and foremost, a conversation about pay and promotion should never be just one conversation – it should be a series of conversations. It's less about a single encounter and more about having a strategic plan for what you want and how you're going to achieve that.

Consider how pay and promotion empower you to be even more effective in your role and your contribution to the organisation. As an example, an elevated job title bolsters your credibility with clients and thus makes them more inclined to do business. It also increases your credibility with suppliers as well as those whom you depend on to execute your responsibilities. Being paid what you're worth enables you to be at your best – you feel motivated, inspired and energised to be a significant contributor to the business. Pay and promotion are *enablers* for your performance. It's not so much about you, but how you can add further value for your manager, colleagues and clients (internal or external) when you're operating at the next level. Begin your difficult conversation with a positive statement or approach. You could give an update on the business and how progress is being made in a given area. You could talk about the things you're enjoying and the things that are going well. Enthusiasm is infectious.

Be your best self

Regardless of the content of the tough conversation, there are a few simple yet effective tips to follow that will dramatically increase your chances of success. It's not necessary to adopt them all – incorporate the pieces that really resonate with you and you feel you can easily embrace. Small steps make a big difference. Thinking about how we want to feel, look, and behave is often overlooked when we're preparing for those tough encounters. This is the best place to start: with you. Bring your best self to the dialogue. This requires a degree of self-awareness. Consider the appropriate timing. When are you in the best mood? When do you feel fresh and inspired? What might be the best timing for the other person? When might they be most receptive to a tough conversation? Being at your best also means being *yourself*. Don't behave in a way that doesn't reflect who you really are and what you believe in because you think that might help the situation. You're hiding the best piece, the piece that enables you to build rapport. If you're being honest, genuine and true to yourself and your values, others will respect you, even if they don't agree with you.

Cultivate an attitude of openness, discovery and curiosity and try to learn as much as possible from the conversation. Attitude is everything. If you go into the conversation thinking you have the whole thing sussed, you're cutting off the opportunity to learn something. This is particularly relevant in feedback conversations. A useful way to kick off a conversation where you're giving feedback could be, 'This is first and foremost a development conversation.' (And of course, you have to mean that in order for it to have the impact you want.) When there is an important piece of negative feedback to share, I like to use the phrase, 'Can I give you some tough love?' If I didn't truly care about the person's development, I wouldn't be taking the time to share feedback with them.

If you're receiving feedback, accept it with an attitude to learn. One of the best ways you can accelerate your professional development is to truly *welcome* feedback. It's a state of mind. When you're looking to solicit feedback on a piece of work or a proposal that you're working on, it's best to follow the 80–20 rule. Don't finish the work to a standard of perfection and then ask for feedback.

I recently caught myself forgetting about this tip in my personal life. My husband and I and our teenage son had signed up for a charity cycle ride. We needed to put together a donation page online. I volunteered to give it a go. I worked hard on it, feeling delighted with the final product. That's where the trouble started – I shouldn't have judged it as the *final* product.

I proudly showed my husband. 'What do you think?'

'Hmm, Zach is really good at this sort of thing. Perhaps we can pass it to him to tidy it up?'

I wanted to explode. What do you mean tidy it up? It's already perfect. Inside, I was feeling angry that my husband hadn't recognised and appreciated my efforts. After a deep breath, I acknowledged he was right. What was I thinking? In retrospect, it was clear that what I should have done was put together a few thoughts and ideas, get feedback from my husband and then ask our son to run with it.

Share the wider context

Framing the conversation or explaining the wider context as to why an issue is important is the best way to shift attention away from you and on to the outcome. When someone smells self-interest, they switch off pretty quickly. Share the bigger picture of what you're trying to do. Others will appreciate that you've taken the time to provide context, enabling them to listen more attentively. It also creates trust, and if they don't trust you, your feedback will fall on deaf ears. Without trust, feedback is immediately discounted. By taking the time to explain the background, you're sending a signal to the other person: 'You're smart. You're worth investing the time in to share the full picture.'

True leaders will often share the bigger picture to inspire others. By doing this, they link the individuals, teams and departments to the wider objective and articulate the role they play in making it reality. Dr Nick Udall in his book *Riding the Creative Rollercoaster* maintains that to attract and retain talent and evoke creativity, productivity and innovation, it's vital to tell the bigger story – a story that values difference and paints an inspiring picture of the future in which we can all see our place and our contribution, where we will feel seen and appreciated. This is how we get others to follow our vision. This is what motivates others to navigate through the difficult conversation – they get a glimpse of what's possible on the other side.

What doesn't kill you makes you stronger

One of the most difficult conversations I've ever had was with my colleague Evan in the early days of my banking career. I had just been hired by the bank to develop the sales and product marketing area for a short-term money market product. One of my briefs was to work with other salespeople in the Fixed Income group to cross-sell my product. The strategy was that the more business the bank did with the same customer, the more likely the customer would stay with the bank. We'd be offering a fuller service. It made sense to me. Evan was a reputable and experienced bond salesperson with enviable client relationships. We had an initial chat about collaborating, but no client visits had yet been arranged. In retrospect, I'm guessing it was because Evan didn't yet trust me. He didn't want to open up his client relationships to a novice.

One day, I was standing next him in front of one of the traders, waiting for their conversation to finish so I could speak to the trader. As I was patiently waiting, Evan turned to me and blurted out, 'What are you doing here? I'm talking to the traders about the market. Surely this is above your head and not very useful.' It felt like I had just been shot. My initial thoughts were, 'What do you mean? Of course, I need to know about the markets in order to sell to my clients. Do you think I don't understand finance and trading? Did you know I have an MBA from a reputable university?' These were the private thoughts in my head. I didn't say a word. I was too stunned to respond. I just walked away, deflated, with my head down.

I knew I had to turn this situation around in order to succeed in my new role. If Evan didn't respect me, the other salespeople wouldn't either and my success depended on them. Though not by title, Evan was in effect a leader, and if he didn't accept me, others would follow his lead. I thought long and hard about what to do. Crying to the boss would make me look weak. That would be like running to the teacher on the school playground because another kid was picking on me. I needed to stand up for myself. I needed to take my destiny into my own hands and sort this out. I needed to gain the respect of my colleagues. Eventually, I decided to arrange a face-to-face meeting with Evan. Oh, how I wished there was another way. There was no other way. Deep breath.

I diligently planned for this daunting conversation. I knew I had to be at my best. I factored in what the best day of the week and time of day would be for me and for Evan. I avoided a Monday or a Friday. On Mondays I was generally tired from the weekend and struggled to get my brain back in gear. On Fridays I was impatient and not creative, having been in high-octane delivery mode for most of the week. Although I am more of a morning person, I realised mornings weren't feasible from a business perspective as that's when the markets are busy and most of the client calls are made. I decided to organise our meet-up near the end of the trading day in the middle of the week.

It was essential that we talked in private, out of respect for Evan and to make sure he didn't lose face in front of his colleagues. Additionally, it needed to be a location where we wouldn't be interrupted. The open trading floor, where we both worked, was out of the question. The atrium, however, would work as it was close to the trading floor and offered a private seating area.

I gathered up the courage and walked over to Evan's desk. 'There's something I'd like to discuss with you. Perhaps we could meet up on Wednesday at 4pm in the atrium. Would that work?'

Evan replied sheepishly, 'Ah, sure, that works. Let's meet then'.

This exuberant, brash salesperson suddenly looked pale and shaken. I certainly was not expecting that. The stage had been set. Between the Tuesday morning when I agreed the meeting with Evan to the actual meeting on Wednesday afternoon, I learned from the traders on my desk that Evan had been snooping around trying to find out what I wanted to talk to him about.

They asked curiously, 'Christine, what is it that you want to chat to Evan about?'

'Nothing interesting for you, I'm afraid,' I countered. I was not sharing this with anyone, not before the discussion, nor after. It was between me and Evan – case closed.

In the planning process, I also considered how I was going to initiate the discussion. It was vital that I looked professional, and that I made it obvious straight away what was in it for him. I wanted to make sure I set the right tone for the conversation. Shaking inside and having slept poorly the night before, I began our chat.

'I think it's important that we work together so that the banks' clients can benefit from a wider range of products. That also means, of course, the more products they trade with us, the more likely we'll be able to retain them as clients. You've been very successful in building up a strong client base, so I'm sure you want to leverage that as much as you can.' I meant that by adding my product, he'd be in a position to better serve and retain his clients.

I intentionally included a compliment in my opening phrase – he had been successful in building up a reputable client list. In the opening I also painted the bigger picture – the clients benefit, he benefits, I benefit, the bank as a whole benefits. It wasn't about me. Although this may all sound logical, it wasn't my first instinct. My first instinct was to attack and go into battle. Allowing time to construct a plan helped calm my nerves and repurpose my anger for gathering up the courage to take on the tough conversation. In preparing I also reminded myself that I had to enter the conversation with the attitude that I didn't understand what was behind his behaviour. I couldn't read his mind. I was prepared to be open and curious about his perspective, and to listen carefully to what he had to say.

The opening phrases did the trick. It was then time to tackle the crux of the issue.

'The reason I wanted to meet up is because I feel that you think I don't know what the f*** a bond is. You need me to be successful and I need you. I didn't appreciate the comments the other day when we were both standing in front of Sam's desk.'

Evan's face turned ashen. He appeared to have been taken completely off guard by my comments. In a humble and measured manner, Evan remarked, 'Christine, I am truly sorry. It was not my intention to insult you.'

I told him that I wanted to keep this between him and me – I had no intention of sharing our conversation with anyone. A look of relief came over his face.

We went on to do record-breaking business together. He opened up his client list. We arranged many joint client visits. We became friends. Our chat took our relationship to a completely new and unexpected level, one I would have never imagined in a million years. While my conversation with Evan was also one of the most formidable of my career, Evan did me a huge favour. He gave me an opportunity to confront a conflict head-on and to achieve a result beyond my wildest imagination. He compelled me to develop a mindset and skill that has served me incredibly well throughout my career. I have been building up that muscle for having tough talks ever since.

As the saying goes, what doesn't kill you makes you stronger. Dealing with conflict head-on became part of my brand. Whenever there was a delicate issue on the trading floor, others sought my advice and often asked me to get involved to achieve a resolution. I noticed that many alpha personalities tended to duck conflict. Possessing the skill and mindset to tackle tough conversations strengthened my character and my brand – in effect, I became an expert at having difficult conversations.

MY ACTION PLAN

1. When approaching difficult conversations, the thing that's holding me back is…

2. My motivation for overcoming this and adopting a more effective approach is…

3. Thinking about an upcoming conversation, my action plan for using this new approach is…

References

Gallo, Amy, 'How to Disagree with Someone More Powerful than You', *Harvard Business Review*, 2016, https://hbr.org/2016/03/how-to-disagree-with-someone-more-powerful-than-you [accessed 22 November 2019].

Gielan, Michelle, *Broadcasting Happiness: The Science of Igniting and Sustaining Positive Change*, unabridged edition, Gildan Media Corporation, 2016.

Kiernan, Kathy, 'Are You Avoiding the Difficult Conversation?', *TEDxSalisbury*, 2016, https://youtube.com/watch?v=exFpUunPoCY [accessed 22 November 2019].

Scott, Susan, *Fierce Conversations: Achieving Success in Work and in Life, One Conversation at a Time*, Piatkus, 2017.

Stichter, Janine, 'How Difficult Conversations Create Growth', *TEDxCosmoPark*, 2019, https://www.youtube.com/watch?v=vPOboi09g4I [accessed 22 November 2019].

Udall, Nick, *Riding the Creative Rollercoaster: How Leaders Evoke Creativity, Productivity and Innovation*, Kogan Page, 2014.

Wekelo, Kerry Alison, *Culture Infusion: 9 Principles to Create and Maintain a Thriving Organizational Culture*, Zendoway, 2017.

Deal With Difficult People

Have you ever felt that your work would be so much easier without certain people? Does it sometimes seem that it's impossible to bring certain individuals on your side and that almost every interaction with them results in a conflict? These difficult characters are everywhere, in every department, company and industry. Like it or not, conflict is a natural part of our daily lives and working virtually certainly doesn't isolate us from similar challenges. One of my most popular webinars ever was entitled 'How to Handle Difficult People'. I had over 1,000 registrations across nearly thirty different countries across Europe, the Middle East, Asia and the Americas. A lot of difficult people are out there, in all parts of the world! They could be a junior colleague, a senior colleague, a boss or a client.

This time my Google research, having typed in the word 'difficult', yielded 'difficult people' straight away. It's clear you're not the only one having challenging conversations or dealing with difficult people. Leaving your organisation is not going to solve the problem. You will come across difficult characters in your new organisation. In fact, you will come across difficult characters in every organisation and every sector, whether private, public or non-profit. They are absolutely everywhere, so the best strategy is to learn how to deal with them. This will be a skill you will use time and again throughout your career.

Behaviour breeds behaviour

You may have heard the saying, 'Your beliefs don't make you a better person. Your behaviour does'. You'd be amazed what happens when you change how you behave. When you change *your* behaviour, others often change theirs, including how they treat you. Human psychology tells us that we can't control others. We can only control how we behave. This includes our response to others' behaviour. The way we behave teaches people how we want to be treated. I liken this to raising kids. You can tell them what to do and what not to do, but if, for example, you tell them smoking is bad for your health, yet you smoke, they are likely to follow your actions rather than your words. If you tell them not to shout, yet you shout (I am guilty of this one!), they discount your words and you lose credibility.

Like parenting, it takes patience and courage to foster good behaviour in ourselves so that we can foster it in others. Effective parenting isn't just barking orders. You've got to *do* what you say. The way we handle ourselves when others treat us poorly can also teach others how to behave. By doing this, we maintain respect for ourselves as well as for the person behaving poorly.

After having recently embarked on a new career in banking, I was stunned when Arthur, one of the traders, referred to me as 'dear'. It wasn't just one time – in every interaction we had, he took the opportunity to call me dear. I'm sure

I was extra sensitive coming from a different culture, but even decades later, I never grew comfortable with this reference in the workplace. I decided that I needed to put a marker down that this was not an appropriate reference to make to a colleague. It felt belittling. I knew I had to collaborate with Arthur on an upcoming client conference I was organising. I reasoned that the best time to raise this issue would be at the end of the day, when the trading floor was quiet and no one would be around. Arthur tended to stay later than the other traders. I prepared the scenario in my head the night before. In addition to his condescending language, Arthur was known for his grumpiness and all-round unpleasant manner. My plan was to launch the conversation talking about the conference and as soon as he let out the first 'dear', I'd make my next move, letting him know that this form of address made me feel uncomfortable. (My feelings were my feelings. You can't argue with someone's feelings.) I'd cite the bigger picture, which was the importance of our good working relationship for the benefit of our team and our clients.

It happened almost exactly as I had imagined. Within minutes, Arthur dropped the D-word. When I proceeded to explain to him that I'd appreciate it if he didn't refer to me as his 'dear' as there was only one guy, my husband, who had earned the right to call me 'dear', Arthur looked bewildered, as if he hadn't realised how often he used this phrase. In any case, he took my comments on board and for the remainder of our time working together he never referred to me as dear again. And I never mentioned our chat with anyone. I was not in the business of undermining others.

The funny thing is, I had almost completely forgotten about this story until I ran into Arthur at a company reunion (celebrating the life of our boss) twenty-five years later. Arthur entered the pub, spotted me straight away and blurted out, 'I'll have you know I've never referred to another woman in the workplace as "dear" since our time together at the bank.' I nearly fell over. I had forgotten about our dialogue. What amazed me is that one conversation with a difficult character had a positive domino effect which I could have never imagined. And I'm not exaggerating when I say Arthur was a difficult character. He continued, 'I want to apologise for my appalling behaviour. Let's set up a lunch – I insist on buying.' That was quite a shock, too, as Arthur had had a reputation for being stingy with his money. We did meet up for a wonderful lunch, during which we caught up on our families; he followed up on his promise and insisted on paying. There's no doubt that this episode twenty-five years prior was a personal development moment for him and for me. Good behaviour breeds good behaviour.

Our behaviour reflects our self-worth. The goal is to adopt an assertive behaviour style when dealing with difficult people. Assertive communication requires us to respect others and respect ourselves. Aggressive behaviour disrespects others. Passive behaviour disrespects ourselves. Assertive behaviour relies on honesty and integrity. It's clear, direct and open communication. It protects your rights and respects those of others. When you behave assertively, you look for solutions that work for both parties. You are forthright about what would make you happy, while balancing the needs of others. Behaving assertively helps develop self-esteem. It's with the difficult characters – whether that be colleagues, bosses or clients – that you want to exhibit assertive behaviour. Assertiveness empowers you to deal effectively with difficult people and work through issues.

Keep your cool

Don't be too hard on yourself. Letting others get under your skin is a natural reaction. It's our ancient brains in operation. We are assessing whether a colleague, boss or client is a friend or foe. As soon as we make that quick assessment that they are a foe, our brain leaps into fight or flight mode. We're under attack. We react. Our bodies are on high alert. Our adrenaline and cortisol spike which impairs our ability to react in a non-emotional, rational way. The aim is to get the front of our brain (the rational part) in gear so we are more in control of the situation. How do we get our brain to make this shift, allowing the logical part of our brain to over-ride the reactive part? One of the simplest ways is to breathe. Breathing is so important, because it assists our mind in settling and taking back control. Breathing allows us to control the pace, pitch and volume of our voice. It allows us to control our tone, ensuring it's congruent with our intention.

When you feel your body tensing up as a result of the interaction with a difficult person, pause and take three deep breaths. Use your breathing as a marker or reminder for you to make sure you're using the right tone for the interaction. Let's face it, dealing with difficult people is stressful, more than getting to grips with technical issues. People are unpredictable and harder to handle. Remember to breathe as you're interacting with that difficult person. In that way, you can dampen your anxiety, control your anger and become more patient. Like so many of my tips and strategies, I find this a useful one to apply in my personal life as well. In dealing with my teenage son (he knows how to press my buttons), I find taking a few breaths allows me to not react and shout back, but rather respond in a way that results in a more productive dialogue. That's a result for any conversation with a teenager.

Another useful tip is to count to five if you're in a pressured situation and you feel like you're under attack. Instead of lashing back, counting to five gives you enough time to calm yourself and to contemplate how to logically respond. That five seconds facilitates the shift from the primitive brain to the rational brain. When I experience my teenage son reacting to situations in a negative way, I remind him, 'Hold it, hold it, count to five. Ok – now respond.' It works to great effect. Counting to five calms him down and his resulting behaviour is more amenable. As behaviour breeds behaviour, my son of course holds me accountable when I exhibit aggressive behaviour (it's a learning process). Time for me to count to five, or to take three breaths. If I forget to apply my own sensible advice, my son is there to remind me. If only colleagues were as forthright.

Listen actively

Listening actively is the cure for so many encounters with difficult people. To show we're listening, nod. One of my favourite ways of showing someone I'm listening is to summarise what they've said, 'I think you're saying...,' or 'What I hear you saying is... Is that correct?' Asking clarifying questions shows others we're listening. Listening *de-escalates* conflict. You're showing the other person you respect them by listening. Listening to understand speaks to our humanity. To be understood makes us feel valued. When it comes to those difficult characters you've been dealing with, how well are you listening? How might you want to listen going forward? Try to figure out why they are difficult. What are their concerns? What do they care about?

Respect the right for other person to have different view. It's not about agreeing with you, but rather finding a solution that works for both parties. Really listening to someone can completely disarm them. I have a live example of this. I was looking to restructure my current TV package. It seemed as if every six months, the cost was going up. That annoyed me so much, it turned my procrastination into action. I thought the conversation was going pretty well with the sales representative who patiently explained the various components of the package and suggested ways it could better suit my needs and reduce in cost. After spending forty-five minutes (of a work day) sorting through the details of the new package, the sales representative concluded, 'You're all set. You've reduced your monthly bill by £30. I'm now going to transfer you to my colleague who will sort out the amended billing.'

I explained to her colleague what had just been negotiated. He announced confidently, 'No, that's a mistake, we can only reduce your bill by £5.' I was livid.

'If there's a mistake, it's your mistake!' I shouted. I hummed and hawed but the second service representative wouldn't budge. I finally yelled,

'Ok, fine, cancel my subscription altogether!' I then spent the rest of the afternoon researching alternative TV packages in the market, motivated by a sense of having been taken advantage of. Hours later, armed with the relevant knowledge, I signed up with another provider, locking in a £30 reduction in my monthly bill.

Unexpectedly, the next day, I received a call from my previous provider. This customer service representative was calling to inquire why I had cancelled the service. Boy, did I give him an earful. He didn't push back on anything I spewed out. He didn't disagree with one single remark. He just listened. Having broken all of my own rules on how to manage difficult people and situations, I had an awakening. I noticed how during this second call, I calmed down completely after my rant. 'How did that happen?' I wondered. Ah, listening – that was the secret. The customer representative had let me vent and he'd listened to every word. He listened so well that he took my complaints and transformed them into new options the company could offer me. I was shocked by how far he was willing to go to keep me as a customer. Listening is powerful. Ultimately, I did transition to my new provider. Given how much research I had done and the amount of time I had spent, I felt too vested in making the change. This incident provided me with two takeaways. The first, a real-life application of how to use listening to deal with a difficult person (in this example, that was me) and second, to not be so quick to make a decision – give others the chance to come back with a counter-offer once the heat has subsided.

Mind your body language

To demonstrate to the other person that you mean what you say, it's important that your body language underpins your positive verbal language. Your body language includes your posture, your head motion, your facial expression, your eye contact and your gestures. Relax your posture, turn your body to the side, and uncross your arms. Nod your head and show a facial expression that indicates you're listening. There's nothing more frustrating than talking to someone who has a sceptical look on their face while you're talking – they give the impression that they're discounting what you're saying and not taking you seriously. I try to remember that look when I'm listening to others. I want to make sure my body language reinforces the message I want to transmit, which is: 'I am truly listening to you.'

Good eye contact is when your gaze meets theirs 60 to 70% of the time. Looking at your watch or your phone negates the message that you're listening. Cognitively, it's not possible to combine the task of listening with looking at your watch or phone. Reflect on the gestures you make when you're listening. Do they have the effect you're hoping? Finger-pointing is a no-no. It can really send others into orbit (perhaps it takes us back to our childhood). The aim is to align all aspects of your body language to be congruent with the message you're trying to convey, whether you're the one speaking or you're the one listening.

Shift the focus to them

Shifting the focus to the other person is especially relevant when you're being put on the spot or someone's finger-pointing and you're caught by surprise. It's also an effective strategy when the other person is angry or being loud or aggressive. By remaining calm, you highlight their bad behaviour. Here are examples of four magic phrases to facilitate the shift from you to them in a way that doesn't sound or feel retaliatory, starting with the phrase 'That's interesting…'

1. Tell me more.

2. Why would you say that?

3. Why would you do that?

4. Why would you ask that?

By using these phrases, you move from being reactive to measured in your response. You're assessing the situation more carefully. You're also buying yourself some time to fully absorb the situation before jumping to a response. In order for these four magic phrases to have the intended impact, it's vital that your tone of voice expresses true curiosity rather than interrogation.

Prepare your response

Responding in a measured manner rather than purely reacting to poor behaviour is where you want to get to when dealing with difficult characters. The above techniques will help you achieve this. To help you respond or react to the trickiest of characters, you'll need to prepare. What have I learned from previous encounters? What is the outcome I'd like to achieve? Visualise it. Occasionally, we're so focused on what we don't want, we forget what we *do* want. When is the next situation I'm likely to encounter the difficult character (or perhaps you want to select a time), and how do I want to respond? Are there any good examples of individuals who seem adept at managing that tricky character? (No need to reinvent the wheel.) What phrases do they use? What body language and tone of voice do they use? There are lots of angles to take into account to help you prepare.

Another role I had in banking required that I interface with the Head of Finance, Patrick. I admired how Patrick kept his cool regardless of how testy and temperamental the traders were. Even when a blame or an insult was catapulted directly at him, he remained cool, calm and collected. As the traders raised their voices, swung their arms and used direct, aggressive language, Patrick simply listened. Perhaps he was feeling the pressure and the stress, but he certainly didn't show it. When I knew a tough meeting was coming up with some challenging individuals, I made sure I was prepared in terms of being well-rested and well-dressed (including wearing a scarf to hide the redness in my neck which would appear uncontrollably when I was stressed). Taking the lead from Patrick, I made a conscious effort to speak in a balanced, calm, and confident way. I noticed that Patrick often asked clarifying questions such as, 'Can you explain why that position is so important and what ramifications it might have for the business?'

Once the trader had explained his position, Patrick would follow up with specific, incisive questions, which would allow him to get to the bottom of the issue. It was amazing to watch. Patrick suffered no fools, as they say. It was clear, however, that through Patrick's speech and body language, he was interested in finding a solution that was sensible for the business. He handled the traders with respect but didn't allow their aggression to hijack the agenda or outcome. Over the many years I worked with Patrick, I never saw him leave a meeting without having achieved a positive outcome or at least a step forward. His composure reinforced his seniority. He looked like the adult in the room. By observing Patrick, I learned to prepare for these encounters. It's not a case of preparing the specific answer, but rather the mindset and

manner necessary to reach the positive outcomes – the win–win – for all present.

You're a busy person. It's not worth your time
to concentrate on every difficult character to
try to improve the situation or relationship.
Be strategic. Focus on the relationships that
will make a difference to you reaching the
long-term goal you're trying to reach. I have
worked with clients who, in preparing for their
promotions, forgot to neutralise the influential
difficult characters who have the power to block
their promotions (even though on paper they
exceeded the so-called metrics required for the
promotion). If someone is truly blocking that
path, you'll need to dedicate time to figuring
out how to deal with this difficult character.
Becoming friends is probably not a realistic
target. The trick is to position your promotion
as benefiting them in some way. By contrast, if
someone is peripheral to what you're trying to
achieve, don't waste your time. Certainly, don't
escalate things, but don't let it absorb your
time. The techniques I've described above will
work in most situations. Having said that, there
are extreme instances where toxic people and
environments are not salvageable and the best
advice is to move on. Toxic individuals and

situations can impact your health and wellbe-ing – nothing is more valuable than that.

MY ACTION PLAN

1. The difficult character I'd like to manage better is…

2. Reflecting on how good behaviour breeds good behaviour, the next time I encounter this difficult character, I'm going to…

3. The other techniques that I am going to use to manage the difficult character are…

References

Allesandra, Tony, 'FAQs – TPR Model of Behav-ior', no date, www.alessandra.com/about _platinumrule/faq.asp [accessed 22 November 2019].

Covey, Stephen R, *The 7 Habits of Highly Effective People: Powerful Lessons in Personal Change*, Free Press, 2004.

Cowley, Jeanette and Brown-Quinn, Christine, 'Resolving Conflict with Head, Heart and Gut', 2019, https://christinebrown-quinn.com/share

-your-story/resolving-conflict-with-head-heart
-gut [accessed 22 November 2019].

Dalley, Deborah, *Developing Your Assertiveness
Skills*, Universe of Learning Ltd, 2013.

Gielan, Michelle, *Broadcasting Happiness: The
Science of Igniting and Sustaining Positive Change*,
Gildan Media Corporation, unabridged edition,
2016.

Markway, Barbara, '20 Expert Tactics for Dealing with Difficult People', *Psychology Today*, 2015,
https://psychologytoday.com/gb/blog/living
-the-questions/201503/20-expert-tactics-dealing
-difficult-people [accessed 22 November 2019].

Ni, Preston, 'Ten Keys to Handling Unrea-
sonable and Difficult People', *Psychology
Today*, 2013, https://psychologytoday.com
/gb/blog/communication-success/201309/ten
-keys-handling-unreasonable-difficult-people
[accessed 22 November 2019].

Ni, Preston, *How to Communicate Effectively and
Handle Difficult People*, Allyn & Bacon, 2002.

Oxman, Murray, *The New, Updated How to Easily Handle Difficult People Handbook*, SWS Publishing, 2012.

Wekelo, Kerry Alison, *Culture Infusion: 9 Principles to Create and Maintain a Thriving Organizational Culture*, Zendoway, 2017.

RULE #9

Tackle Tricky Tensions

While there are difficult *people* whom we need to have specific strategies to deal with, we equally need to be prepared to tackle tricky *situations* in order to successfully navigate our careers. Life would be so much simpler if we could just focus on the job, but this isn't reality. Knowing how to handle tricky situations will empower you to navigate any organisation, in any sector (annoying human behaviour is inescapable – it exists in all organisations, sectors and geography). Have you ever wondered, 'What's the best way to say no? How do I stand my ground when I'm under direct attack? How do I make requests without sounding too pushy on the one hand, but unassertive on the other?' The tricky situations that come up repeatedly tend to be ones where we should be saying no, but that's problematic for a whole host of reasons, which we'll turn to shortly. Disagreeing with a client, colleague or boss is equally challenging. When making a request, it can also be a struggle to get the balance right between sounding pushy on the one hand and weak or wimpy on the other.

Evaluate what to say yes to

The question that requires proper evaluation is when you should say yes or no. Not all situations are equal. What criteria should be used to evaluate the right answer for you? There isn't a universal right answer. It depends. What's your overarching career goal, direction or strategy? Where do you want to get to? It's within that framework that you can properly assess the various scenarios that may arise. Knowing what to say yes to gives you control of your career and helps you shape it.

Let's say you want to become a director in your company. Stepping up to that level of seniority in any company or sector will require you to enhance your visibility. Your ability to do the job well is a given. At this level, it's crucial that your talents and hard work are seen. By knowing your career strategy or direction, you can then develop your 'what to say yes to' strategy. Through that filter, evaluate *who* are the people you should say yes to. Say yes to those people who are going to directly facilitate your progression or who could give you the right support to make that happen.

Through that same filter, evaluate *what* you should say yes to. What are the things that would support your developmental goals? You want to be involved in topics, projects and activities that are going to be instrumental in helping you achieve your goals. Let's face it, you're overstretched as it is – it's impossible to say yes to everything. You don't need to feel guilty about that. It's not your fault that there are only twenty-four hours in a day. Not all tasks, activities or projects hold equivalent value. Choose the ones that suit you best. As an example, the *what* could comprise your involvement in more client-facing work, which may in turn increase your visibility within your organisation, another top priority.

Sandra is an auditor for one of the London-based banks. A senior colleague specially requested her to lead an audit for Risk Management. While the content of the audit didn't necessarily provide a stretch opportunity for Sandra, the chance to lead (and get credit for leading) the audit was a stretch opportunity. Furthermore, the senior colleague who made the request also happened to be instrumental in supporting Sandra's business case for her promotion to director. The audit fit in with her goal to increase her visibility inside and outside the Audit group, a development point which had been raised by her manager during a recent performance review. Leading the audit was also congruent with Sandra's 'what to say yes to' strategy. She was clear what she needed to get out of the opportunity while meeting the needs of the department she was working in. Notice how this opportunity didn't necessarily tick all the boxes – ie, the content of the audit wasn't a stretch for her. However, the other benefits were valuable enough to Sandra that she decided to say yes.

When you're asked to do something you're not thrilled about, but you know you can do and do well, seize the moment to say what kind of work you *want* to be involved in. In a subtle way, you're making an agreement. Sandra followed up with her senior colleague, 'Yes, I'd like to lead the proposed audit. I wanted to also let you know that I'm very interested in leading an audit for one of the global businesses should that opportunity arise.' Depending on the circumstance, you can also use humour to make the point that you'll help out now in exchange for their help later (quid pro quo). There were times in my banking career when I did agree to do things I preferred not to, but I valued the relationship and was prepared to do a favour. In those instances, I'd respond jokingly, 'Yes, I can do that for you, but you're going to owe me one.' It wasn't clear to me what exactly I was going to come back and ask for, but I knew eventually something would come up.

Beware of the downside of not saying no

Beware of the downside of not saying no. It's a slippery slope. Eventually it catches up with you and can box you into a corner. The biggest downside of not saying no is that we can get sidelined. We think we're going to just do this one thing and then we'll get back on track with the things that are strategically important to moving our careers forward. This rarely happens, as we unwittingly get sucked into other people's agendas. Staying focused on what's going to contribute to success in our current role as well as facilitate our growth and progression requires us to be intentional about which activities, projects or tasks we choose to be involved in. You could work twenty-four hours a day and still not complete everything. It's crucial to prioritise the activities that truly will have an impact on the outcome you're seeking.

Another downside of not saying no is that we can develop a reputation for becoming the dumping ground for others. 'Oh, he or she is always so helpful. Give it to them. I'm sure they'll do it.' While it's useful to have a reputation for pitching in and being a good team player, if you're not careful, you can get labelled as that doer who gets trapped in the same role for a long time. I've been there. I used to think that the more tasks I could execute, the more valuable I'd become to an organisation. That plan backfired. Even if you could do every task assigned to you, plus the tasks you've agreed to take on for others, you won't get promoted. You become the helper who is always there but never gets credit for delivering strategically important work. We can make ourselves look more junior by the type of work we agree to take on. By not setting boundaries, others don't respect us and frankly, we don't show respect for ourselves.

Focus on the outcome rather than the approach

You position yourself as a leader by focusing on outcomes rather than being wedded to a specific tactical approach. This is the stuff leadership is made of. You motivate your team by providing them the space to develop their own ideas on how to reach the desired outcome. This allows for creativity, innovation, and most importantly for the team to take full ownership of the approach. They have a vested interest in making sure their method works. They have bought into the idea by virtue of it being theirs in the first place.

When we disagree with someone, we tend to focus on our differences and forget to acknowledge where there is commonality. That's an example of low-level listening: 'I'm only listening so I can tell you what I disagree with'. When working in cross-cultural, competitive and ambitious teams, I find that reiterating and reconfirming the outcome we're all trying to get to helps reset everyone's attention. It's not about what I think, or you think, but rather what approach or mix of approaches will help us achieve that common goal we agree we're striving for. In a disagreement, people can often become emotionally wedded to a certain view and forget about what they're trying to achieve. Their objective is simply to get others to agree with their view. When you encourage others to shift the attention to the common goal, you're also sending a message that that's what you care about. No self-interest is at play here.

Useful phrases to dampen disagreements

Think of a few examples of recent disagreements. Going forward, you may find it helpful to use the following phrases to move a dialogue to a mutually beneficial outcome:

- I think I may have a different perspective. From where I sit, I see...

- I don't agree with *all* the points you've made. I do appreciate, though, how honest you've been and the care and time you've taken to share your view.

- I recognise we haven't had the same experience. For completeness' sake, the experience I've had is…

- I believe we're on the same page with where we want to get to. Let's see if we can agree an approach that works for both of us and the team.

- I recognise that there's more than one approach to solve the problem. I think we can agree that the bigger goal we both want to get to is…

- Let's chat through how we can make that happen… (where there's consensus or buy-in from the team).

Crafting an effective request

I know what you're wondering: 'Christine, this is business. Who has time to think about how to make a request? When I'm asking others to do things, especially direct reports, I want them to just do it!' I completely relate to that sentiment. What I've learned is that to get the best out of others, you've got to figure out how to motivate them. While commanding others to do things may work in the short term, it's unlikely to result in happy, productive teams in the long run. In today's highly matrixed, global teams, it's also increasingly likely that we make requests to someone who doesn't report to us and who has a separate line manager and agenda.

Requests are most powerful when they are delivered using positive language. Avoid, therefore, apologising or playing the victim. No need to apologise. You've done nothing wrong and it undermines the validity of your request. No one likes the victim mentality. We tend to switch off when others say, 'I have so much to do. I worked such long hours this week,' or, 'I have this deadline and that deadline.' No one likes a whiner. You won't win any popularity contests at work with an 'I'm a victim' attitude. Stick to the facts of the matter. No one likes it when they feel they're being manipulated through flattery or little white lies. We don't trust people like that. White lies eventually catch up with you and damage your reputation. Make requests in a way that you'd like others to do so. Treat others as you'd want them to treat you.

We often fall in the trap of trying to soften the blow by using indirect language which lacks specifics. We then wonder why the other person hasn't done what we've asked. Have we been clear and specific enough? Instead of asking, 'Is there any chance someone could get the reports done asap?' you could, for instance, be more specific: 'Could you produce the sales reports by close of business on Friday?' Others will be thankful for the clarity of the request. They will know what's involved and what's expected.

Make your requests motivational

Taking the time to explain the wider business context does wonders for our motivation. When this happens, we feel like we matter. We feel like someone respects us and values us enough not to just bark orders at us. Providing the larger business context also creates an environment where we can develop. Understanding the meaning of things can lead to new ways of doing things. When others bark orders at us, we are made to feel like children again – doing things without understanding.

Continuing with the example above, you could say that the reason you're asking for the sales reports is that the results are going to be discussed at next week's Monday management

meeting. During that meeting, some key decisions will be made about where best to allocate
resources. With that background, the person
you're asking to generate the report is able to
consider the needs of the audience and what
might be useful to analyse or highlight. Making
requests is also an opportunity for others to
grow. Perhaps the person you're asking has
never done sales reports before. This could be
a chance for them to branch out and develop
their knowledge and skills. Be sure to share that
perspective. You might also mention that it's a
chance for them to raise their profile. The report,
which will be distributed to the leadership team,
will have their name on it.

We're so busy moving on to the next thing that
needs to be delivered, we often forget to say
thank you and provide feedback to the person
who has fulfilled the request. Taking the time
to say thank you or for giving feedback is fundamental to motivating and developing others.
After the management meeting you could say,
'It was a tough management meeting, but the
clarity of your reports really helped us zero in
on the right data to make sensible decisions.'
You may also have constructive feedback to
share, such as, 'I'd like to share with you in
more detail how the report was used in the

meeting. Let's put some time in the diary to discuss that, so that you have the full picture. You may want to tweak the report going forward based on this additional insight.'

When you share context and background, don't be surprised if you're presented with alternative ideas and suggestions. Be open. What most surprised me when I shared with my team the bigger picture is that they had better ideas about how to fulfil a request or tackle a problem. They would point out that a similar issue had been raised before and there was no need to do what I was asking. There was a better, faster way. While you may have ideas about how to do things given your experience, empower those around you to generate their own ideas and suggestions. They will be more motivated to help you fulfil your requests.

Despite your best efforts, the reply to your request might be no. Be ready to hear no. Try to leverage the interaction with this other person to help you solve the issue. If you get a no, take this opportunity to ask, 'Who else might be able to do it? Is there another approach that would be more efficient?' Use that interaction as a resource to get closer to solving the problem. Perhaps there's a more appropriate person who can help you. Perhaps there's an alternative path for achieving the outcome you're looking for.

Raising awkward issues

In these complex settings we operate in, awkward issues are bound to arise. When raising an awkward issue, choose an appropriate time (for you and the other party) and a private area. Set the scene by providing the facts. Explain the impact on you (if necessary) and the business. Finally, discuss a solution.

In one of my corporate senior roles, I was responsible for approving expenses of the ten other managing directors who were part of the management team. I remember receiving an expense claim for an internal team dinner from one of the managing directors, Joseph. The team had certainly had a terrific year, but the cost of the dinner was more than they had ever spent on one before. Something didn't sit right. This would be a delicate situation, as Joseph ran the most profitable trading area in the division. The head of the division (my boss) would not be happy if I pissed the guy off. Equally, my boss would not be happy if I didn't instil discipline and respect for internal policies and procedures. It was a rock and hard place scenario for sure. The worst approach I could take would be to simply confront Joseph with how ridiculous his reimbursement request was (although that's certainly how I felt).

Instead, with the help of his personal assistant, I booked fifteen minutes with Joseph in his office the end of the trading day. I entered his office, closed the door and explained the facts:

'Joseph, I wanted to discuss this expense claim for the internal dinner you hosted earlier this month. The cost per head is about three hundred pounds. That's substantially above what we've reimbursed other managers.'

'Ah, I see, how does it normally work?'

'Well, you may know that we're under a lot of scrutiny from the head office to reduce expenses. What I've agreed with the head of our division is that the firm reimburse fifty pounds per head, the remainder to be funded personally by the team members or the head of the desk.'

'No problem, Christine. I will pick up the remainder personally. Thanks for bringing this to my attention.'

Had I approached Joseph with a condescending attitude or raised this issue in front of his team, it could have resulted in an unpleasant situation and the expense issue may have remained unresolved. This process works well regardless of whether the person you're addressing the awkward issue with is more senior than you. Given that you will feel more stressed when you're engaging in the conversation, it's worth spending a few minutes preparing in your head how the scenario might play out. Practise how you're going to articulate the facts, the impact and the proposed solution.

Standing your ground

Know when to stand your ground. When is it important to make sure your view is not ignored? Be selective about which battles to fight. If you fight every battle, you're unlikely to win as you'll be spread too thinly. Also, others will start to predict that you're going into battle mode as usual, and they will ignore you – 'There they go again.' On the other hand, if the situation is one in which one of your underlying principles is at stake, you should stand your ground. If your view is about an inconsequential issue, you may want to compromise. You will lose credibility if you stand your ground for every single issue. You'll develop the reputation that you're just stubborn, and others will learn to work around you.

In one of my sales and marketing roles (in an institution that no longer exists), a senior trader and former boss asked to look at the details of one of my potential client's portfolio holdings. The problem was that the area I worked in then had a fiduciary responsibility *not* to share that information with the trading arm of the bank. This relates to so-called 'Chinese Walls' that protect clients' interests. We both knew, of course, that analysing the details of the portfolios could help him with his trading strategies.

'Stanley, you and I both know that would be breaching client confidentiality.'

Stanley was persistent. I had to learn how to say no in numerous ways. Eventually, he stopped asking, but it was an experience I'll never forget. Standing your ground really goes to the heart of who you are and what you want to be known for.

MY ACTION PLAN

1. These are the things that I should be saying no to and the things I should be saying yes to…

2. The situation I want to better manage is…

3. The phrase(s) that could be useful in navigating this situation are…

4. The bigger picture I want to share is…

5. My overall approach that I will follow to tackle this tricky situation is…

References

Cialdini, Robert B, *Influence: The Psychology of Persuasion*, revised edition, Harper Business, 2007.

Dalley, Deborah, *Developing Your Assertiveness Skills*, Universe of Learning Ltd, 2013.

Eblin, Scott, 'Why Leaders Should Focus on Outcomes Instead of Solutions', 2017, https://eblingroup.com/blog/leaders-focus-on-outcomes [accessed 22 November 2019].

Goulston, Mark and Ullmen, John, 'How to Really Understand Someone Else's Point of View', *Harvard Business Review*, 2013, https://hbr.org/2013/04/how-to-really-understand-someo [accessed 22 November 2019].

Teitel, Amy Shira, 'How Groupthink Led to 7 Lives Lost in the Challenger Explosion', *History.com*, 2019, https://history.com/news/how-the-challenger-disaster-changed-nasa [accessed 22 November 2019].

Thomas, Clarence, *My Grandfather's Son: A Memoir*, reprint edition, HarperCollins, 2008.

RULE #10

Manage Your Manager

One of the most important relationships in our careers is the relationship we have with our boss. And let's face it, with the dominance of matrix reporting, global operations and incessant restructurings, that manager may change more frequently than we'd like. And worse yet, we may have *several* bosses that we need to keep happy at the same time and who may sit in different locations as well as time zones. According to *Inc.* magazine, three out of four employees report that their boss is the most stressful part of their job. Like other aspects of your career, it's up to you to take control of this relationship rather than be passive and let it control you. How actively do you manage your relationship with your boss?

Own the relationship

If you had told me when I entered the work-force in my early twenties that it was my job to manage my boss, I would have thought you were mad. Aren't we paid to do our jobs rather than to manage the boss? My younger self believed that it was the sole responsibility of the boss to manage the relationship. The boss is more senior and would know more about how to do that sort of thing. Duped by the myth that 'doing a good job' was the be-all and end-all, the thought of managing the boss would have never crossed my mind. It wasn't until well into my thirties that I realised no matter how hard I worked, no matter how smart I was, I was never going to progress unless I learned how to manage my manager.

Yes, I'm familiar with the counter-arguments: 'But Christine, it's my boss's job to think about how to develop me and develop our relation-ship. Isn't that what he or she is paid for? I resent this is my responsibility.' When I first started working with Meera, a software developer, she repeated this logic several times. Meera's objection was well-articulated: 'Twenty-five percent of my boss's compensation is dependent on how well the boss develops and manages me.'

I countered, 'That's the stated policy. How much do you *really* think your boss's compensation is determined by how well you're developed?'

Meera sighed and then replied despondently, 'In actual fact, although this is technically how compensation is calculated, the reality is the boss's compensation is almost exclusively tied to revenue targets, regardless of the other targets.'

Why was I continuing to (gently) push Meera to take ownership of this relationship? Even though all the points Meera raised were technically accurate, my telling her she was in the right was not going to help the situation. I shared some tough love instead. The reality is that the most effective relationships are *not* passive. My younger self believed that the boss was all-knowing and perfect, which led me to behave passively. There's no doubt this slowed my career progression and often left me feeling frustrated, ignored and demotivated. It's dangerous to assume that the boss magically knows what information or help their subordinates need and that they will automatically provide it. This assumption leads to unrealistic expectations and constant disappointment. Don't sit back and wait. Own and manage the relationship with your manager.

Raises, promotions and high-profile projects depend directly on how well you manage your boss. Managing your boss effectively *enables* you to do your job well. It's not extra. Without their support, buy-in, guidance and trust, no matter how hard you work, things will continue to be a struggle. This was certainly the case for my client Kristin. Kristin works for a global technology consulting firm, and despite being held at the current level of Senior Manager for several years longer than normal, she is aiming to become Managing Director. The first step in the process is that your reporting manager puts forward your name. Kristin was devastated to learn that she didn't even make this first hurdle. Her boss intentionally held back her promotion this year.

Through our conversation, Kristin realised that her boss was supportive of her promotion, but felt she wasn't 100% ready. In this type of scenario, the boss's reputation is also on the line. Bosses don't want to stick their necks out unless they are reasonably confident the promotion will get approved. The other discovery for Kristin was that she needs to carefully manage the boss to gain the support she requires. Throughout this chapter I'll be referring to Kristin to share how she is bringing her boss on side to secure her promotion to Managing Director next year. For the first time ever, Kristin feels in control and on track to secure support for her promotion based on direct feedback from her boss as well as other key influencers at her company.

Make your boss successful

Make sure you understand your boss and his or her world. What are the challenges and pressures that he or she faces? What are the boss's goals and objectives – from a personal point of view as well as from a corporate point of view? Hilary (the accountant I mentioned in the first chapter who successfully transitioned to a role in industry) makes a conscious effort to help her manager manage his stakeholders. Whenever she produces a financial report, white paper or status report for a specific technical topic, she crafts it in a way that makes it easily accessible to a more senior audience. She understands how they prefer to see information.

Hilary is also sensitive about her manager's preferred work style – his strengths, weaknesses and blind spots. (We all have blind spots). Her boss's blind spot is people management, which happens to be one of Hilary's strengths. She has become one of her boss's trusted advisors when it comes to making decisions about people. She sees things her boss doesn't see. She has a good sense of how to motivate others. Her boss appreciates and values Hilary's contribution, notably in the areas where he is weak and she is strong. Not spending time understanding the boss is like flying blind. Working hard without understanding the boss results in that hard work being ignored, misplaced and easily forgotten.

No matter what your role is, your number one priority is to make your boss successful. Regardless of what it says on your job description, your top priority is *always* to make your boss successful. When you do this, that success is likely to be mutual. To make bosses successful, it's essential to figure out what success looks like *for them*. Kristin was looking for guidance on how to approach her manager about transitioning her role from day-to-day caretaking to managerial oversight of a major client. At the same time, she wanted to take on two smaller client projects. Her thinking was that this would provide her with the management experience she needed to reach Managing Director. We spent an entire hour getting into the head of the boss. I encouraged Kristin to really think about what her boss cares about. What's his mantra? What is he always going on about?

'Ah,' exclaimed Kristin, 'He's always going on about the client. What does the client think? What does the client care about? He says the client should be at the centre of everything we do.'

'That's it!' I exclaimed. We then worked through how to present her proposal by starting with how each of the three clients would be well served through her suggested arrangement. By framing her conversation in this way, the boss would be inclined to listen.

Before approaching the boss, Kristin already had discussions with the clients, in a soft way, about her level of involvement. Her sense was that each of the clients was happy with the potential arrangement. Kristin felt that each of her client teams were also well-placed for the proposed level of her involvement. She had been working hard over many months to get her team to step up so that she could be less hands-on. Kristin later reported that the meeting with her boss went swimmingly. Kristin's boss had been impressed that Kristin was taking ownership of her career development. He welcomed the proposed change to her client portfolio, as it would give her the leadership and management experience she was lacking (which her boss had highlighted previously). The boss even commented: 'Kristin, there's something different about you.'

Show interest in your boss's career. To make yourself invaluable, you should deliver what your boss needs before your boss knows he or she needs it. Learn how to predict those needs by expressing curiosity about your boss's experience and perspective. You will then be able to predict what's needed when.

The three most powerful questions

Understanding the boss requires some investigation. Here are the three most powerful questions to gain insight into your boss's core concerns:

1. What are your priorities and how can I help you achieve them?

2. How involved do you want to be in this particular area?

3. How do you want me to communicate with you?

These questions will certainly get the boss's attention. They help to understand expectations and clarify communication. You're sending a clear message to your manager – 'I care about my career. I care about doing a good job. I'm taking ownership of my role and my career.' These are all positive messages to be sending the boss. At the beginning of a new role or project, or when working with a new manager or boss, the most powerful question is: 'What does success look like for my role, in six months or in a year from now?

Understand yourself

Understanding the boss is step one. Step two is understanding yourself. What are *your* key needs and your goals? What pushes your buttons? Kristin realised that she was too passive in her behaviour towards her boss. This is what she perceives to be behind her boss's comment that she seemed 'different'. Kristin wasn't previously taking ownership of her career and tended to just go along with things. She was quite happy letting others make suggestions and following them. What makes you tick? Consider the following:

- Your strengths and weaknesses

- Your values and principles

- Your personal style when you're operating at your best

To build a strong relationship with your manager, it's *not* necessary for you to change who you are. Simply by understanding where any differences or conflict lie, you'll be better prepared to work through those differences. With your new-found understanding, you can detach yourself from the emotion. This will enable you to maintain your confidence level and use your logic to determine how to best manage any conflicts. Kristin was able to flex her style (rather than change who she is fundamentally) to be more outspoken and assertive.

This required a concerted effort and practice. It didn't come naturally for Kristin. By flexing her style, Kristin gained the confidence of her boss. Whatever skill or talent you're seeing in others that appears natural, trust me, it's not. They've been practising hard to make it look that easy.

Approach your relationship as a partnership

By approaching your relationship with the boss as a partnership, you'll gain the respect of your boss and others. Your reputation in the organisation will be enhanced. A partnership approach meets your needs and style as well as those of your boss. It is characterised by *mutual* expectations. It's a relationship in which you keep the boss informed and is based on dependability and honesty. You've asked the boss how he or she likes to work. Take the opportunity to share with the boss how *you* like to work and be managed in order to deliver your best work. Since all bosses have a default management style, it's up to you to help your boss understand how he or she can help you do your best. This requires both self-awareness and the courage to speak up. Cultivate both, then have the conversation. The conversation isn't about making demands for your needs, but rather showing a genuine interest in supporting your boss in the best way possible. The boss, by understanding your requirements for being at your best, is in effect helping you help them.

Your relationship with the boss is a two-way street and a three-way win. The two-way street refers to the *mutual* dependence between you and your manager. The boss needs your help and co-operation to do their job effectively, and vice versa. Think more broadly about how the boss can help you. Managers, for example, can link you to the rest of the organisation. They can raise your profile by giving you exposure to others outside of your department. They can help you understand and set priorities and secure the resources you need to do your job well.

Bosses are adept at understanding the bigger picture and how you fit into it. I have always found that the boss's perspective on the polit-ical environment was always invaluable – who's who, and who do I need to keep happy (so-called stakeholders, formal *and* informal). That's the type of information you won't find printed anywhere. You, on the other hand, are in the unique position of hearing and seeing things that the boss can't, by virtue of being less senior. You can be the eyes and ears of the boss in terms of what's happening at the ground level of the organisation. You may also become aware of political threats to the boss. Giving the boss a heads up on this type of information is invaluable. The boss will appreciate that you're watching his or her back, and that favour is likely to be reciprocated. When your boss succeeds, you succeed, and the organisation succeeds – that's a three-way win.

Managing conflict – agree to disagree

Being adept at managing conflict with the boss is part and parcel of doing your job. It's not a 'nice-to-have'. A relationship between any two individuals is bound to throw up conflict. Each of us has our own needs, styles, personalities, etc, and therefore we should *expect* conflict. In relation to the boss, the key is to *nurture* a conflict in a way that enhances and deepens the dialogue. Avoid losing control of a conflict, as this damages the relationship. Avoiding conflict altogether, however, makes you look weak and more junior. It's a delicate balancing act for sure. Pick your battles carefully. Not all points of conflict are worth resolving. In any case, in some circumstances, such as under time constraints, it might be necessary to go with the boss's suggestion after all.

If you see your boss about to make a poor decision, suggest a better alternative. However, once your boss has made that decision, stop second-guessing and do your best to implement it, regardless of whether you agree (assuming their decision is ethical, legal, etc). The boss will gain more confidence in you when he or she sees that your suggestions are insightful. If what you suggested turns out to have been the better option, it's best not to gloat by saying, 'I told you so'. The boss will remember and appreciate it if you don't come back and rub their face in it.

Focus on the *outcome* the boss wants. This is what you need to agree on. It's easy to get caught up with differences in the tactics. Maintaining the focus on the outcome the boss wants will result in them being more relaxed on the 'how' or the approach. I am a realist. There are bosses out there who behave badly. Bad behaviour is a form of communication. Something is bothering them. When a boss misbehaves, reflect on the potential cause – and don't take it personally.

Most managers get almost no leadership training and little support. What's prompting the boss's bad behaviour? How might you be able to help them?

Establish mutual expectations

In light of the fast-moving workplace environment, it's always worth confirming and reconfirming expectations. Try to avoid making assumptions. Double-checking takes seconds. Going down the wrong path can take months to rectify. As mentioned earlier, the relationship with the boss is two-way and involves mutual expectations. Expectations can be implicit or explicit. Most bosses do not spell out their expectations in detail. What they say and what they mean could be two completely different messages. You'll need to put your detective hat on again. In many organisations there will be a formal process for communicating expectations as part of career-planning reviews or performance reviews. Invariably, these systems aren't perfect. (A number of large companies are beginning to disband these practices.) Circumstances and expectations can change considerably between the occasions these formal review processes take place.

My client Annabel shared with me a comment from her new boss that really provided the backdrop to their working relationship. The boss commented, 'If you leave this group within two years, you have failed me and the company. If you don't have a new role or challenge after two years, the company (and me as your manager) have failed you.' This set a clear expectation around how long the new boss expected her to be in her role. The powerful question of 'What does success look like?' is well-suited to gain clarity about expectations in a way that is vivid and practical. The best time to have that conversation is *before* you start a new role or project.

Once you understand expectations, you're in a better position to understand what resources you might need to meet them. I use the word 'resources' in the broadest sense – they could mean working from home one day a week, having access to admin support, or to certain individuals, which would require the boss making some introductions. Do speak up if your manager seems confused or misinformed about your role, goals, etc. Clearing up any misunderstanding sooner rather than later will allow you to address the discrepancies *before* your performance is viewed as unsatisfactory.

One of the most annoying parts of the formal appraisal process is when you learn *during* the appraisal process that you were supposed to be focusing on something else. If only you had known. This happened to me once and I realised I needed to be continually confirming and reconfirming expectations with my boss and other key stakeholders to avoid it happening again.

Kristin continues to invest in her relationship with the boss. As part of the leadership team, Kristin's manager will be tasked with helping the firm reposition itself to solve wider industry problems, not just deliver technology solutions. Kristin's interest lies in the Life Sciences, especially fertility. She is working hard to increase her profile in fertility innovation and build alliances across the firm. This is her wow factor. Rather than being an operational technologist, Kristin is a strategic thinker who looks at technology as a medium to make transformational change. She shares her enthusiasm and thirst for innovation with clients, who may have initially hired the firm to roll out technology software to operational efficiencies but are now struggling with how to leverage technology to transform their business model.

Kristin's efforts to build a personal brand in Life Sciences make her boss look good. Her brand-building embellishes his individual brand as well. Kristin has recently been nominated for an internal leadership programme, largely due to her profile-building in this cutting-edge area. Kristin's boss expects her to be building her profile in this way. Although we refer to it as 'self-promotion', we're actually promoting the talents of our boss in developing and guiding us as well. Our success is their success. Kristin expects the support of her boss in preparing her for promotion to Managing Director, while her boss expects her to step up and lead conversations about innovation in Life Sciences throughout the organisation.

MY ACTION PLAN

1. To understand the boss better, I am going to…

2. To understand myself better, I am going to…

3. To adopt and invest in a partnership approach with the boss, I am going to…

References

Eblin, Scott, 'How to Get Your Micromanager Boss to Back Off', 2019, https://eblingroup.com/blog/micromanager-boss [accessed 22 November 2019].

Forbes Coaches Council, '15 Ways to Get Your Boss to Stop Micromanaging You', 2018, https://forbes.com/sites/forbescoachescouncil/2018/01/10/15-ways-to-get-your-boss-to-stop-micromanaging-you [accessed 22 November 2019].

Gabarro, John J and Kotter, John P, 'Managing Your Boss', *Harvard Business Review*, 2005, https://hbr.org/2005/01/managing-your-boss [accessed 24 November 2019].

Higson, Phil and Sturgess, Anthony, 'Manage Your Boss – 8 Ways to "Manage Up"', *The Happy Manager.com*, no date, https://the-happy-manager.com/articles/manage-your-boss [accessed 24 November 2019].

Karlgaard, Rich, '12 Easy Ways to Manage Your Boss', *Forbes.com*, 2014, https://forbes.com/sites/richkarlgaard/2014/06/14/12-easy-ways-to

-manage-your-boss/#6fb5008c1a55 [accessed 24 November 2019].

Mahoney, Steve, 'How to Handle Micromanaging Bosses', *Monster.com*, no date, https://monster.ca/career-advice/article/handling-micromanaging-bosses [accessed 24 November 2019].

Ryan, Liz, 'How to Manage Your Boss – Ten Dos And Don'ts', *Forbes.com*, 2018, https://forbes.com/sites/lizryan/2018/01/28/how-to-manage-your-boss-ten-dos-and-donts/#4362be373142 [accessed 24 November 2019].

Tulgan, Bruce, 'How Do You Manage the Boss If You Work in Different Locations?' *Monster.com*, no date, https://monster.com/career-advice/article/managing-boss-remote-location [accessed 24 November 2019].

Final Thoughts

You've done it. You've unlocked the gateway to your success by discovering the unwritten rules to career progression. You now know how to position yourself so that your skills and talents receive the recognition they deserve. You are fully equipped and ready to take the actions that will truly make a difference to your career progression and fulfilment. As you've worked through the chapters, you may have come to appreciate that the rules are mutually reinforcing. As you learn one rule, you're discovering how it can support the mastering of other rules. Advancing your career isn't necessarily easy but taking the *right* small steps can make a big difference. Mastering the unwritten rules leads to a shift in mindset and behaviour that changes everything. You are firmly in the driving seat for advancing and shaping your career.

The workplace is in a state of flux and constant disruption, which throws up many challenges. Those challenges, however, are also what open up opportunities for you to make your mark and fulfil your true potential. Grab those opportunities. By aligning your skills and talents to the needs and challenges of the organisation or industry you want to impact, you are well-placed to create your unique path. Others will want to listen to your ideas and suggestions, as you're framing them in a way that addresses *their* problem. You only have one life – shape it in a way that works for you both personally and professionally. Continue to invest in yourself – you're worth it. When you're at your best, everyone wins – your colleagues, friends, family and the communities where you live. And finally, enjoy life's trials and tribulations. Without them, life would be boring. You only fail when you don't try. An exciting ride is there for the taking.

Acknowledgements

As always, thanks to my number one fan, husband and soulmate, Tom, for encouraging me to continue to write. I am also thankful for the expert advice and professional guidance from the team at Rethink Press.

Last but not least, I am grateful for all the feedback from clients who have inspired me to take the time to write down those tricky little unwritten rules that can derail the most promising careers.

The Author

Following nearly thirty years in the corporate world, Christine Brown-Quinn, aka The Female Capitalist®, embarked on a new career in 2010 to share with aspiring professional women across the world practical, hands-on business strategies to fast-track their careers (the stuff they don't teach in business school). She's also been on a mission to bust the myth that a rewarding career and a fulfilling personal life have to be at loggerheads.

Through her webinars, one-on-one coaching and in-person workshops, Christine unveils what really matters when it comes to getting ahead in demanding corporate environments. As a former managing director in international finance, Christine is well versed in what it takes to forge a thriving career in highly pressurised, alpha environments.

If you think you could benefit from one-on-one coaching or participating in a career strategy programme, contact Christine at:

✉ christine@christinebrown-quinn.com
🌐 www.christinebrown-quinn.com
in https://uk.linkedin.com/in
    /christinebrownquinn
🐦 @FemaleCapital

Also By This Author

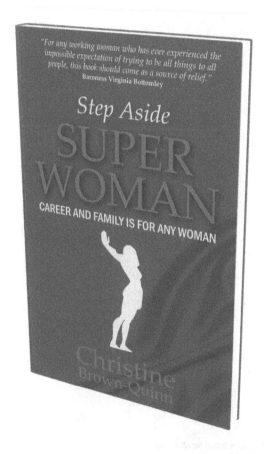

"For any working woman who has ever experienced the impossible expectation of trying to be all things to all people, this book should come as a source of relief."
Baroness Virginia Bottomley

Step Aside

SUPER
WOMAN

CAREER AND FAMILY IS FOR ANY WOMAN

Christine
Brown-Quinn

CPSIA information can be obtained
at www.ICGtesting.com
Printed in the USA
FSHW021457080320

9 781781 334416